Database Repairing and Consistent Query Answering

Synthesis Lectures on Data Management

Editor
M. Tamer Özsu, *University of Waterloo*

Synthesis Lectures on Data Management is edited by Tamer Özsu of the University of Waterloo. The series will publish 50- to 125-page publications on topics pertaining to data management. The scope will largely follow the purview of premier information and computer science conferences, such as ACM SIGMOD, VLDB, ICDE, PODS, ICDT, and ACM KDD. Potential topics include, but not are limited to: query languages, database system architectures, transaction management, data warehousing, XML and databases, data stream systems, wide scale data distribution, multimedia data management, data mining, and related subjects.

Probabilistic Ranking Techniques in Relational Databases
Ihab F. Ilyas and Mohamed A. Soliman
2011

Uncertain Schema Matching
Avigdor Gal
2011

Fundamentals of Object Databases: Object-Oriented and Object-Relational Design
Suzanne W. Dietrich and Susan D. Urban
2010

Advanced Metasearch Engine Technology
Weiyi Meng and Clement T. Yu
2010

Web Page Recommendation Models: Theory and Algorithms
Sule Gündüz-Ögüdücü
2010

Multidimensional Databases and Data Warehousing
Christian S. Jensen, Torben Bach Pedersen, and Christian Thomsen
2010

Database Replication
Bettina Kemme, Ricardo Jimenez Peris, and Marta Patino-Martinez
2010

Relational and XML Data Exchange
Marcelo Arenas, Pablo Barcelo, Leonid Libkin, and Filip Murlak
2010

User-Centered Data Management
Tiziana Catarci, Alan Dix, Stephen Kimani, and Giuseppe Santucci
2010

Data Stream Management
Lukasz Golab and M. Tamer Özsu
2010

Access Control in Data Management Systems
Elena Ferrari
2010

An Introduction to Duplicate Detection
Felix Naumann and Melanie Herschel
2010

Privacy-Preserving Data Publishing: An Overview
Raymond Chi-Wing Wong and Ada Wai-Chee Fu
2010

Keyword Search in Databases
Jeffrey Xu Yu, Lu Qin, and Lijun Chang
2009

Database Repairing and Consistent Query Answering
Leopoldo Bertossi

ISBN: 978-3-031-00755-2   paperback
ISBN: 978-3-031-01883-1   ebook

DOI 10.1007/978-3-031-01883-1

A Publication in the Springer series
SYNTHESIS LECTURES ON DATA MANAGEMENT

Lecture #20
Series Editor: M. Tamer Özsu, *University of Waterloo*
Series ISSN
Synthesis Lectures on Data Management
Print 2153-5418   Electronic 2153-5426

Database Repairing and Consistent Query Answering

Leopoldo Bertossi
Carleton University, Ottawa, Canada

SYNTHESIS LECTURES ON DATA MANAGEMENT #20

ABSTRACT

Integrity constraints are semantic conditions that a database should satisfy in order to be an appropriate model of external reality. In practice, and for many reasons, a database may not satisfy those integrity constraints, and for that reason it is said to be *inconsistent*. However, and most likely a large portion of the database is still semantically correct, in a sense that has to be made precise. After having provided a formal characterization of consistent data in an inconsistent database, the natural problem emerges of extracting that semantically correct data, as query answers.

The consistent data in an inconsistent database is usually characterized as the data that persists across all the database instances that are consistent and minimally differ from the inconsistent instance. Those are the so-called *repairs* of the database. In particular, the *consistent answers* to a query posed to the inconsistent database are those answers that can be simultaneously obtained from all the database repairs.

As expected, the notion of repair requires an adequate notion of distance that allows for the comparison of databases with respect to how much they differ from the inconsistent instance. On this basis, the minimality condition on repairs can be properly formulated.

In this monograph we present and discuss these fundamental concepts, different repair semantics, algorithms for computing consistent answers to queries, and also complexity-theoretic results related to the computation of repairs and doing consistent query answering.

KEYWORDS

integrity constraints, inconsistent databases, database repairs, consistent query answering, data cleaning

To Prof. Jöerg Flum,
for his guidance, support, an example of scholarship,
relentless research activity, and humanity

Contents

Preface

A common assumption in data management is that databases can be kept *consistent*, that is, satisfying certain desirable integrity constraints (ICs). This is usually achieved by means of built-in support provided by database management systems. They allow for the *maintenance* of limited classes of ICs that can be declared together with the database schema. Another possibility is the use of *triggers* or *active rules* that are created by the user and stored in the database. They react to updates of the database by notifying a violation of an IC, rejecting a violating update, or compensating the update with additional updates that restore consistency. Another common alternative consists of keeping the ICs satisfied through the application programs that access and modify the database, i.e., from the transactional side.

However, under different circumstances and for several reasons, databases may be or may become inconsistent. For example, ICs that are expensive to check and maintain, enforcement or simple consideration of new or user ICs, imposition of a new semantics on legacy data, the creation of a repository of integrated data, etc. Confronted to the possible or potential inconsistency of a database, we may decide to live with this inconsistency, but trying to access, retrieve and use the portion of data that is still consistent with respect to the ICs under consideration.

Consistent query answering (CQA) [Arenas et al., 1999] emerged from this attitude towards inconsistency and the need to do semantically correct data management, in particular, query answering, in the presence of inconsistency. This required a precise, formal characterization of the consistent data in a possibly inconsistent database, and also the development of computational mechanisms for retrieving the consistent data, e.g., at query answering time.

The characterization of consistent data, as first proposed by Arenas et al. [1999], appeals to the auxiliary notion of *database repair*. This is a new database instance that is consistent with respect to the ICs, and *minimally differs* from the inconsistent database at hand. Consistent data is invariant under the class of possible repairs. Since their official inception, CQA has received much attention from the research community in data management. The main problems mentioned above, i.e., characterization of consistent data and the development of efficient algorithms, have been largely explored. The former under different notions of repair (and distance between instances), and the latter, considering all kinds of combinations of classes of ICs and queries, including complexity-theoretic issues.

In this monograph we introduce the motivation, the main concepts and techniques, and also the main research problems that appear behind and around database repairs and CQA. Much research has been produced and published in the last 12 years. It would be impossible to give a detailed account of it in a rather short monograph like this. As a consequence, the treatment of most of the topics and research results is kept rather intuitive and superficial, but hopefully still precise enough. We have preferred illustrative and representative examples to full proofs of theorems. However, we have provided abundant references to the publications where those results can be found in full detail, and much more. Some surveys of the area have been published before [Bertossi, 2006, Bertossi and Chomicki, 2003, Chomicki, 2007].

This monograph concentrates on CQA and database repairs in/for single relational databases. As a consequence, some topics in CQA and repairs for other data models have been omitted. Some of them are mentioned below.

Consistent query answering and repairs for *XML databases* have been considered by Flesca et al. [2005a,b] and Staworko and Chomicki [2006]. The same problems in *multidimensional databases* (MDDBs), but with semantic constraints like *homogeneity* and *strictness*, have been considered by Bertossi et al. [2009], Bravo et al. [2010] and Ariyan and Bertossi [2011], on the basis of the Hurtado-Mendelzon model for MDDBs [Hurtado and Mendelzon, 2002]. And for *spatial databases*, by Rodriguez et al. [2008, 2011].

Consistent query answering and database repairs has been applied in *virtual data integration systems* that are subject to global integrity constraints [Bertossi and Bravo, 2004b, Bravo and Bertossi, 2003, 2005]. They have also played an important role in *peer data exchange systems* that exchange data at query answering time when certain data exchange constraints between peers are violated. In consequence, inconsistency is the driving force behind data movement between peers [Bertossi and Bravo, 2004a, 2007, 2008].

We are not presenting here research on *probabilistic* representation of repairs or repairs in *probabilistic databases* [Andritsos et al., 2006, Lian et al., 2010] (except for general remarks in Section 6.2.1).

Leopoldo Bertossi
August 2011

Acknowledgments

I am indebted to many people who have made writing this monograph possible. Special thanks go to my several coauthors of papers on consistent query answering, database repairs, and data cleaning. It has been a stimulating, enriching and pleasant experience working with them.

I am especially grateful to Jef Wijsen, Ihab Ilyas, and Solmaz Kolahi for their help with contributed material to this monograph. Also to Filippo Furfaro and Franceso Parisi for personal conversations and some useful material on their research. Valuable and detailed comments and suggestions by Jan Chomicki to a first version of this monograph are very much appreciated. Of course, in the end I am the only one responsible for any errors introduced, and also for the choice of subjects and the way they are presented.

I am grateful to Tamer Özsu for the opportunity to write this monograph, and his suggestions for improving it. Interacting with Tamer is always a pleasure.

My warmest thanks go to my wife, Jennifer, and my daughter, Paloma, for all the support, patience, and love I have received from them during all the time, several years by now, that I have spent doing research in the area.

Leopoldo Bertossi
August 2011

CHAPTER 1

Introduction

A database can be seen as a model, i.e., as a simplified and abstract description, of an external reality. In the case of relational databases, one starts by choosing certain predicates of a prescribed arity. The *schema* of the database consists of this set of predicates, possibly *attributes*, which can be seen as names for the arguments of the predicates, together with an indication of the domains where the attributes can take their values. Having chosen the schema, the representation of the external reality is given in terms of relations, which are finite extensions for the predicates in the schema. This set of relations is called an *instance* of the schema.

For example, a relational database for representing information about students of a university might be based on the schema consisting of the predicates *Students*(*StNum*, *StName*) and *Enrollment*(*StName*, *Course*). Attribute *StNum* takes numerical values; *StName*, values that are finite character strings; and *Course*, values that are alphanumeric strings. Figure 1.1 shows a possible instance for this schema.

Students	StuNum	StuName		Enrollment	StuNum	Course
	101	john bell			104	comp150
	102	mary stein			101	comp100
	104	claire stevens			101	comp200
	107	pat norton			105	comp120

Figure 1.1: A database instance.

1.1 DATABASE CONSISTENCY

In order to make the database a more accurate model of the university domain (or to be in a more accurate correspondence with it), certain conditions are imposed on the possible instances of the database. Those conditions are intended to capture more meaning from the outside application domain. In consequence, these conditions are called *semantic constraints* or *integrity constraints* (ICs). Already in the classical and seminal paper by E.F. Codd [Codd, 1970] on the relational data model it is possible to find the notions of integrity constraint and consistency of a database.

For example, a condition could be that, in every instance, the student name functionally depends upon the student number, i.e., a student number is assigned to at most one student name. This condition, called a *functional dependency* (FD), is denoted with *StUNumber* → *StName*, or

Students : *StuNumber* → *StuName*, to indicate that this dependency should hold for attributes of relation *Students*. Actually, in this case, since all the attributes in the relation functionally depend on *StuNum*, the FD is called a *key constraint*.

Integrity constraints can be declared together with the schema, indicating that the instances for the schema should all satisfy the integrity constraints. For example, if the functional dependency *Students* : *StuNumber* → *StuName* is added to the schema, the instance in Figure 1.1 is *consistent*, because it satisfies the FD. However, the instance in Figure 1.2 is *inconsistent*. This is because this instance does not satisfy, or, what is the same, violates the functional dependency (the student number 101 is assigned to two different student names). Functional dependencies form a particular class of integrity constraints.

Students	StuNum	StuName		Enrollment	StuNum	Course
	101	john bell			104	comp150
	101	joe logan			101	comp100
	104	claire stevens			101	comp200
	107	pat norton				

Figure 1.2: An inconsistent instance.

With the same schema, it is also possible to consider a *referential integrity constraint* requiring that every student (number) in the relation *Enrollment* appears, associated with a student name, in relation *Students*, the "official table" of students. This is denoted with *Enrollement*[*StNum*] ⊆ *Students*[*StNum*]. If this IC is considered in the schema, the instance in Figure 1.1 is inconsistent, because student 105 does not appear in relation *Students*. However, if only the referential constraint were considered with the schema, the instance in Figure 1.2 would be consistent.

As we can see, the notion of consistency is relative to a set of integrity constraints. When we say that a database is inconsistent, it means that the particular instance of the database at hand is inconsistent, and wrt the given ICs.

The two particular kinds of integrity constraints presented above, and also other forms of ICs, can be easily expressed in the language of first-order (FO) predicate logic [Enderton, 2001], which in relational databases usually takes the form of the *relational calculus* [Abiteboul et al., 1995]. For example, the FD above can be expressed by the symbolic sentence

$$\forall x \forall y \forall z ((Students(x, y) \wedge Students(x, z)) \longrightarrow y = z), \tag{1.1}$$

whereas the referential constraint above can be expressed by

$$\forall x \forall y (Enrollment(x, y) \longrightarrow \exists z\, Students(x, z)). \tag{1.2}$$

Notice that this language of FO predicate logic is determined by the database schema, whose predicates are now being used to write down logical formulas. We may also use "built-in" predicates, like the equality predicate. Thus, ICs can be seen as forming a set Σ of sentences written in a language of predicate logic.

A database instance can be seen as an *interpretation structure D* for the language of predicate logic that is used to express the ICs. This is because an instance has an underlying domain and (finite) extensions for the predicates in the schema. Having the database instance as an interpretation structure and the set of ICs as a set of symbolic sentences is crucial, and makes it possible to simply apply the notion of satisfaction of a formula by a structure of first-order predicate logic [Enderton, 2001]. In this way, the notion of satisfaction of an integrity constraint by a database instance is a precisely defined notion: the database instance D is consistent if and only if it satisfies Σ, which is commonly denoted with $D \models \Sigma$. We will be more precise about ICs and their satisfaction in database instances in Chapter 2, Section 2.1.

Since it is usually assumed that the set of ICs is consistent as a set of logical sentences, in databases the notion of consistency becomes a condition on database instances. Thus, this use of the term "consistency" differs from its use in logic, where consistency characterizes a set of formulas.

Inconsistency is an undesirable property for a database. In consequence, one attempts to keep it consistent as it is subject to updates. There are a few ways to achieve this goal. One of them consists in declaring the ICs together with the schema, and the database management system (DBMS) will take care of the database maintenance, i.e., of keeping it consistent. This is done by rejecting transactions that may lead to a violation of the ICs. For example, the DBMS should reject the insertion of the tuple (101, *sue jones*) into the instance in Figure 1.1 if the FD (1.1) was declared with the schema (as a key constraint). Unfortunately, commercial DBMSs offer limited support for this kind of database maintenance.

An alternative way of keeping consistency is based on the use of triggers (or active rules) that are stored in the database. The reaction to a potential violation is programmed as the action of the trigger: if a violation is about to be produced or is produced, the trigger automatically reacts, and its action may reject the violating transaction or compensate it with additional updates, to make sure that in the end, consistency is reestablished. Consistency can also be enforced through the application programs that interact with the DBMS. However, the correctness of triggers or application programs with respect to (wrt) ensuring database consistency is not guaranteed by the DBMS.

1.2   AN APPETIZER AND OVERVIEW

In practice, it is the case that databases may be or become inconsistent. That is, they may violate certain ICs that are considered to be relevant to maintain for a certain application domain. This can be due to several reasons, e.g., poorly designed or implemented applications that fail to maintain the consistency of the database, ICs for which a DBMS does not offer any kind of support, ICs that are not enforced for better performance of the DBMS or application programs, or ICs that are just assumed to be satisfied based on knowledge about the application domain and the kind of updates on the database.

It is also possible to have a legacy database on which semantic constraints have to be imposed; or more generally, a database on which imposing new constrains depending on specific needs, e.g., user constraints, becomes necessary.

In the area of data integration the satisfaction of desirable ICs by a database is much more difficult to achieve. One can have different autonomous databases that are separately consistent wrt their own, local ICs. However, when their data are integrated into a single database, either material or virtual, certain desirable global ICs may not be satisfied. For example, two university databases may use the same numbers for students. If their data are put together into an integrated database, a student number might be assigned to two different students.

When confronted to an inconsistent database, the application of some *data cleaning* techniques may be attempted, to cleanse the database from data that participates in the violation of the ICs. This is done sometimes. However, data cleaning is a complex and non-deterministic process; and it may also lead to the loss of information that might be useful. Furthermore, in certain cases, like virtual data integration, where the data stays at the autonomous data sources, there is no way to change the data without ownership of the sources.

One might try to live with an inconsistent database. Actually, most likely one will be forced to keep using it, because there is still useful information in it. It is also likely that most of the information in it is somehow consistent. Thus, the challenge consists in retrieving from the database only information that is consistent. For example, one could pose queries to the database at hand, but expecting to obtain only answers that are semantically correct, i.e., that are consistent with the ICs. This is the problem of *consistent query answering* (CQA).

The notion of consistency of a database is a holistic notion, that applies to the entire database, and not to portions of it. In consequence, in order to pursue this idea of retrieving consistent query answers, it becomes necessary to characterize the consistent data in an inconsistent database first. The idea proposed by Arenas et al. [1999] is as follows: the consistent data in an inconsistent database are those that are invariant under all possible ways of restoring the consistency by performing minimal changes on the initial database. That is, no matter what minimal consistency restoration process is applied to the database, the consistent data stay in the database. Each of the consistent versions of the original instance obtained by minimal changes is called a *minimal repair*, or simply, a *repair*.

As expected, one has to be more precise about the meaning of minimal change. In between, several definitions have been proposed and studied in the literature. They are usually given in terms of a distance or partial order between database instances. Which notion to use may depend on the application. In the rest of this section we will illustrate the concept of minimality associated to repairs as originally introduced in [Arenas et al., 1999], using our previous example, with the FD.

First of all, a database instance D can be seen as a finite set of ground atoms (or database tuples) of the form $P(\bar{c})$, where P is a predicate in the schema, and $\bar{c}$ is a finite sequence of constants in the database domain. For example, *Students*$(101, john bell)$ is an atom in the database. If the admissible repairs actions are insertions or deletions of full tuples (as opposed to changes of attribute values), which we will assume for now, a natural way to compare the original database instance D

with any other database instance D' (with the same schema) is through their symmetric difference $D \Delta D' = \{A \mid A \in (D \setminus D') \cup (D' \setminus D)\}$.

In this setting, restoring consistency wrt to a functional dependency can be achieved only through tuple deletions. In consequence, if D' is obtained from D by eliminating tuples, the symmetric difference becomes simply $D \setminus D'$. Instance D' is considered to a be a minimal repair of D if D' satisfies the FDs, and is set-theoretically maximally contained in D, i.e., there is no consistent D'' with $D' \subsetneq D'' \subsetneq D$.

For example, the database in Figure 1.2 has two repairs wrt the FD (1.1), those shown in Figure 1.3. Each of them is obtained by deleting one of the two conflicting tuples in relation *Students* (relation *Enrollment* does not change). This notion of repair and also alternative definitions of repair are introduced in detail and discussed in Chapter 2, Sections 2.3 and 2.5.

Students1	StuNum	StuName
	101	john bell
	104	claire stevens
	107	pat norton

Students2	StuNum	StuName
	101	joe logan
	104	claire stevens
	107	pat norton

Figure 1.3: Two repairs.

Having defined the notion of repair, a *consistent answer* from an instance D to a query $\mathcal{Q}(\bar{x})$ wrt a set Σ of ICs is defined as an answer $\bar{c}$ to $\mathcal{Q}$ that is obtained from every possible repair of D wrt Σ. That is, if the query $\mathcal{Q}$ is posed to each of the repairs, $\bar{c}$ will be returned as a usual answer to $\mathcal{Q}$ from each of them.

For example, if the query $\mathcal{Q}_1(x, y)$: *Students*(x, y), asking for the tuples in relation *Students*, is posed to the instance in Figure 1.2, then (104, *claire stevens*) and (107, *pat norton*) should be the only consistent answers wrt the FD (1.1). Those are the tuples that are shared by the extensions of *Students* in the two repairs. Now, for the query $\mathcal{Q}_2(x)$: $\exists y$ *Students*(x, y), i.e., the projection on the first attribute of relation *Students*, the consistent answers are (101), (104) and (107). Consistent query answers are defined in precise terms in Chapter 2, Section 2.3.

There might be a large number of repairs for an inconsistent database. In consequence, it is desirable to come up with computational methodologies to retrieve consistent answers that use only the original database, in spite of its inconsistency. Such a methodology, that works for particular syntactic classes of queries and ICs, was proposed by Arenas et al. [1999].

The idea is to take the original query $\mathcal{Q}$, that expects consistent answers, and syntactically transform it into a new query $\mathcal{Q}'$, such that the *rewritten query* $\mathcal{Q}'$, when posed to the original database, obtains as usual answers the consistent answers to query $\mathcal{Q}$.

For illustration, we can use our example. The consistent answers to the query $\mathcal{Q}_1(x, y)$: *Students*(x, y) above wrt the FD (1.1) can be obtained by posing the query

$$\mathcal{Q}'(x, y): \textit{Students}(x, y) \wedge \neg \exists z (\textit{Students}(x, z) \wedge z \neq y) \tag{1.3}$$

to the database. The new query collects as normal answers from the initial instance those tuples where the value of the first attribute is not associated to two different values of the second attribute in the relation. It can be seen that the set of answers for the new query can be computed in polynomial time in the size of the database.

In this example, a query expressed in first-order predicate logic was rewritten into a new query expressed in the same language. A central question is about the scope of first-order rewritability. As expected, it depends on the kind of query and ICs involved. Actually, it has limited applicability, because it can be proved that for certain FO queries and ICs, no FO rewriting exists. This is not surprising, considering the complexity-theoretic results already available in the literature. Actually, for certain classes of FO queries and ICs, deciding if a tuple is a consistent answer can be Π_2^P-complete (in the size of the database instance). This strongly suggests that the decision problem cannot be solved in polynomial time, which would be the case if there was a FO rewriting for the query. First-order query rewriting is presented in Chapter 3. Limitations of first-order query rewriting and complexity-theoretic issues are discussed in Chapter 5, for different kinds of repair semantics.

In consequence, the next question is about a more expressive language than FO logic that can be used to express the rewriting Q' of the first-order query Q. The answer to this question should also depend on the kind of ICs being considered. For example, it may be necessary to do the rewriting as a query written in a more expressive extension of Datalog [Abiteboul et al., 1995, Ceri et al., 1989]. More expressive languages for query rewriting are investigated in Chapter 4.

If a database is inconsistent wrt referential ICs, like the instance in Figure 1.1 and the constraint in (1.2), it is natural to restore consistency by deleting tuples or inserting tuples containing *null values* for the existentially quantified variables in the ICs. For example, the tuple (105, *comp120*) could be deleted from *Enrollment* or, alternatively, the tuple (105, *null*) could be inserted in relation *Students*. This requires a modification of the notion of repair and a precise semantics for satisfaction of ICs in the presence of null values. As indicated above, different repair semantics, that include those that allow for the use of null values, are described in Chapter 3, Section 2.5, and Chapter 4, Section 4.1.4.

Repairs were originally introduced as an auxiliary concept to define consistent query answers. However, they have gained a life of their own. Computing a repair for a database that violates certain semantic constraints can be seen as a form of data cleaning. In Chapter 6 we explore this connection.

1.3   OUTLOOK

As we will see in the rest of this monograph, a considerable amount of research has been done in the area of database repairing and consistent query answering. By now we have a reasonably good understanding of the applicability of query rewriting approaches, and a rather clear view of complexity issues, at least for certain common classes of integrity constraints and queries. For some of them we even have polynomial time algorithms for CQA, and also some efficient and good approximation algorithms for some intractable cases. Of course, there are still many interesting open problems in the area, including still many problems about FO query rewriting and computational complexity in general.

If we want to see the concepts and techniques that have been developed for CQA widely adopted and used, we should address other open problems that have received little attention so far. One of them turns around *compositional methods for CQA*. That is about the possibility of computing consistent answers to a query by composing the sets of consistent answers to subqueries. Notice that CQA does not follow the classical logical laws that apply to (usual) query answering in relational databases. CQA follows a different, non-classical logics. This issue is raised and discussed in Chapter 4. The importance of better understanding the *logic of CQA* is the reason for having introduced most of the material in it.

Another important open problem is related to CQA in a dynamic setting, when the database is subject to updates. We need *incremental techniques* for computing repairs and doing CQA, i.e., that avoid computing everything from scratch after the updates. Instead, we should be able to reuse and minimally change an already available repair or an existing set of consistent answers. For usual data management on relational databases we have incremental techniques for view maintenance and verification of integrity constraints. This kind of methodology is still undeveloped for database repairing and CQA.

Another problem that clearly emerges from the subjects treated in the monograph consists in *shedding a more clear light on the repair semantics* that are suitable for different kinds of applications. Admittedly, this problem is rather vaguely formulated, but that does not make it less relevant. Research in this direction should combine experience from concrete applications with the, possibly comparative, study of general properties of different repair semantics.

This brings us to another but related problem, namely the development of *key applications* of database repairing and CQA. Applications to virtual data integration systems subject to global ICs look particularly promising, because there CQA seems to be the way to go.

CHAPTER 2

The Notions of Repair and Consistent Answer

2.1 PRELIMINARIES

We will consider relational schemas of the form $\mathcal{S} = (\mathcal{U}, \mathcal{R}, \mathcal{B})$, where $\mathcal{U}$ is the possibly infinite database domain; $\mathcal{R}$ is a finite set of database predicates, each of them with a fixed finite arity; and $\mathcal{B}$ is a finite set of built-in predicates, e.g., $\mathcal{B} = \{=, \neq, >, <\}$. For an n-ary predicate $R \in \mathcal{R}$, $R[i]$ denotes the ith position or attribute of R, with $1 \leq i \leq n$. If an attribute A is associated to a position, $R[A]$ denotes predicate R restricted to that position. The schema determines a language $L(\mathcal{S})$ of first-order (FO) predicate logic. A relational instance D for schema $\mathcal{S}$ can be seen as a finite set of ground atoms of the form $R(\bar{a})$, with $R \in \mathcal{R}$, and $\bar{a}$ a tuple of constants from $\mathcal{U}$.

Queries are formulas of $L(\mathcal{S})$. In particular, we will consider *conjunctive queries*. They are of the form:

$$\mathcal{Q}(\bar{x}) : \exists \bar{y} (R_1(\bar{x}_1) \wedge \cdots \wedge R_n(\bar{x}_n) \wedge \varphi), \tag{2.1}$$

where $R_i \in \mathcal{R}$, $\bar{x}, \bar{y}, \bar{x}_i$ are finite sequences of variables, with $\bar{x} \subseteq \bigcup_i \bar{x}_i$, and $\bar{y} = (\bigcup \bar{x}_i) \setminus \bar{x}$.[1] Formula φ is a conjunction of built-in atoms containing variables or domain constants, and its variables appear all in some $R_i(\bar{x}_i)$. The variables in $\bar{x}$ are the free variables of the query. Their combined values in $\mathcal{U}$ that, together with the instance D, make the formula defining the query true are the *answers to query* $\mathcal{Q}$ in D. If $\bar{x}$ is of length n, we say that the query is n-ary. When the query is defined by a sentence, i.e., it has not free variables (e.g., $\bar{x}$ is empty in (2.1)), its arity is 0, and we call it a *boolean* (conjunctive) query.

To indicate that a sequence $\bar{c}$ of elements of $\mathcal{U}$ is an answer to the query $\mathcal{Q}$, we write: $D \models \mathcal{Q}[\bar{c}]$, i.e., instance D satisfies the query when the variables in $\bar{x}$ take the values as in $\bar{c}$. $\mathcal{Q}(D)$ denotes the set of answers to query $\mathcal{Q}$. When the query is *boolean*, $\mathcal{Q}(D) = \{yes\}$ if the sentence is true in D, and $\mathcal{Q}(D) = \{no\}$, otherwise.

Views are predicates defined by a formula of $L(\mathcal{S})$. $V(D)$ denotes the extension of view V when computed on an instance D for $\mathcal{S}$.

---

[1]When there is no possible confusion, we treat sequences of variables as set of variables. I.e. $x_1 \cdots x_n$ as $\{x_1, \ldots, x_n\}$.

Integrity constraints (ICs) are sentences of $L(\mathcal{S})$. When an instance D satisfies an IC ψ, we write $D \models \psi$. If Σ is a set of ICs, $D \models \Sigma$ means that all the ICs in Σ are satisfied by D. In that case, we say that D is *consistent* (wrt Σ). Otherwise, we say it is *inconsistent*.

Example 2.1 Consider the relational database schema $\mathcal{S}$ with $\mathcal{R} = \{R(A, B), S(B, C)\}$. Here, A, B, C are attributes. This is a possible instance for this schema: $D = \{R(a, b), R(c, d), R(c, g), S(b, c), S(d, c), S(e, a)\}$.

Consider the unary view V defined by the sentence $\forall x (V(x) \equiv \exists y \exists z (R(x, y) \wedge S(y, z)))$. This is a *conjunctive view* since it is defined by the conjunctive query: $\mathcal{Q}(x) : \exists y \exists z (R(x, y) \wedge S(y, z))$, the one on the right-hand-side of V's definition. In this case, $V(D) = \{(a), (c)\}$, and, of course, $\mathcal{Q}(D) = \{(a), (c)\}$.

A possible integrity constraint is $\psi : \forall x \forall y \forall z (R(x, y) \wedge R(x, z) \rightarrow y = z)$. This is a *functional dependency* (FD) of the second attribute of R upon the first; also denoted $R : A \rightarrow B$. Actually, it is trivially a *key dependency* (KD), in the sense that the combination of the attributes on the LHS of the arrow functionally determines all the other attributes of the predicate.

ICs can be written in different syntactic forms, depending on what we want to do with them. For example, the FD above can also be written in *clausal form*: $\forall x \forall y \forall z (\neg R(x, y) \vee \neg R(x, z) \vee y = z)$. Here, $\neg R(x, y)$ is a *negative literal*, i.e., the negation of an atom (atomic formula). Atoms are positive literals. The same FD can also be written as a *denial constraint*: $\forall x \forall y \forall z \neg (R(x, y) \wedge R(x, z) \wedge y \neq z)$, i.e., as a prohibition of a particular combination of database atoms and built-ins.

Instance D is inconsistent, because it does not satisfy the FD, which is denoted with $D \not\models \psi$. The tuples $R(c, d)$, $R(c, g)$, combined, violate the FD.

However, D does satisfy the *referential constraint* $\chi : \forall x \forall y (S(x, y) \rightarrow \exists z R(y, z))$. Thus, in this case, $D \models \chi$. It is easy to prove that this (actually, any) referential constraint cannot be written as a denial constraint. ∎

We will always consider finite sets IC of integrity constraints in a language $L(\mathcal{S})$. We will assume these sets are *logically consistent*, in the sense that there is an instance D with $D \models IC$.

Generalizing the previous example, and for future reference, we provide the following definition.

Definition 2.2 (a) A *universal constraint* is an $L(\mathcal{S})$-sentence that is logically equivalent to one in clausal form, i.e., of the form:

$$\forall \bar{x} (L_1(\bar{x}_1) \vee \cdots \vee L_n(\bar{x}_n) \vee \varphi(\bar{x}'))\,,$$

with: $\bar{x} = \bigcup \bar{x}_i$, $\bar{x}' \subseteq \bar{x}$, $\varphi(\bar{x}')$ a disjunction of atoms with built-in predicates, and each $L_i(\bar{x}_i)$ is a literal of the form $R(\bar{x}_i)$ or $\neg R(\bar{x}_i)$, for $R \in \mathcal{R}$.

(b) A *denial constraint* is an $L(\mathcal{S})$-sentence (that is logically equivalent to one) of the form

$$\forall \bar{x} \neg (A_1(\bar{x}_1) \wedge \cdots \wedge A_n(\bar{x}_n) \wedge \varphi(\bar{x}'))\,,$$

with: $\bar{x} = \bigcup \bar{x}_i$, $\bar{x}' \subseteq \bar{x}$, $A_i(\bar{x}_i)$ is a database atom (i.e., with predicate in $\mathcal{R}$), and φ is a conjunction of atoms with built-in predicates.

(c) An *inclusion dependency* is an $L(\mathcal{S})$-sentence of the form

$$\forall \bar{x}(R(\bar{x}) \rightarrow \exists \bar{y} S(\bar{x}')) \,,$$

with $\bar{x}' = \bar{y} \cup \bar{z}$, $\bar{y} \cap \bar{z} = \emptyset$, $\bar{z} \subseteq \bar{x}$. When $\bar{y}$ is empty, we skip the existential quantifier. ∎

As mentioned in Example 2.1, functional and key dependencies belong to the class of denial constraints. Referential constraints belong to the class of inclusion dependencies. For additional material on database fundamentals, see [Abiteboul et al., 1995].

2.2   CONSISTENT DATA IN INCONSISTENT DATABASES

Under certain circumstances, we may have to live with inconsistent data, with information that contradicts certain desired integrity constraints (ICs). This is the case, for example, when: (a) a DBMS does not fully support data maintenance, i.e., integrity checking or enforcing; (b) the consistency of the database will be restored by executing additional, compensating transactions, or future transactions; (c) integration of semantically heterogeneous databases, without a central or global maintenance mechanism; (d) there is inconsistency wrt to "soft" or "informational" integrity constraints that we hope or expect to see satisfied, but they are not necessarily maintained; (e) we have user constraints than cannot be checked; or (f) we inherit legacy data and we want to impose some new semantic constraints on them.

Restoring consistency may be difficult, impossible, or even, undesirable: We may not have the permission to do so. We may not want to lose potentially useful data. Furthermore, restoring consistency can be a computationally complex and non-deterministic process. We may also need some absent additional domain knowledge to do some sort of data cleaning.

A more flexible approach is based on the observations that: (a) not all data participate in the violation of the ICs, actually, possibly most of the data are semantically correct; and (b) the database can still give us semantically correct answers to (some) queries. In consequence, we may try to live with inconsistency.

However, if we decide to go this way, we should be in position to tell apart consistent from inconsistent data. The former should be formally characterized. More precisely, we should be able to provide a precise definition of consistent data in a possibly inconsistent database. In particular, this notion should be applicable to query answers.

After such a characterization is achieved, the next step should be the development of algorithms for obtaining such consistent information from the inconsistent database. However, the success of such a task will be determined by the intrinsic computational complexity of the problem, which we have to investigate and understand.

Query answering in relational databases follows a classical logic. In particular, it follows some useful compositional laws, in the sense that the answers to a query can be determined on the basis of the answers to its sub-queries. However, obtaining consistent answers to queries from inconsistent databases may follow a different logic, that we should identify and investigate.

In order to motivate our basic concepts, we will revisit the example shown used in Chapter 1.

Example 2.3   Consider the following database instance D. We expect the functional dependency *FD*: *StuNum* $\rightarrow$ *StuName* to be satisfied. However, D violates *FD*, by the tuples with value 101 for attribute *StuNum*.

D	Students	StuNum	StuName
		101	john bell
		101	joe logan
		104	claire stevens
		107	pat norton

There are several ways to restore consistency, and two crucial issues appear: (a) What kind of operations will be allowed to do that? (b) How much do we want to depart from the given inconsistent instance?

Trying to stay as close as possible to the given instance is quite natural. However, the first issue, of how to change the given instance, is less obvious. For the moment, we will accept only full tuple insertions and deletions as possible operations. With them, and trying to minimally change the given instance, we find only two possible alternative and consistent instances, namely:

D_1	Students	StuNum	StuName
		101	john bell
		104	claire stevens
		107	pat norton

D_2	Students	StuNum	StuName
		101	joe logan
		104	claire stevens
		107	pat norton

These two instances are consistent wrt the FD, and they stay close to D. Now we observe that the tuple (104, *claire stewens*) persists in all repairs, which is not surprising since it does not participate in the violation of *FD*. Actually, this tuple is invariant under these minimal ways of restoring consistency.

On the other side, the tuple (101, *joe logan*) does not persist in all repairs, which is related to the fact that is does participate in the violation of *FD*.   ∎

Notice that the notion of integrity constraint satisfaction applies to the database instance as a whole. That is, the database either satisfies a given set of integrity constraints *IC* or it does not. Whereas here we want to characterize the *consistency of portions of data* in an inconsistent database. The previous example suggests how to proceed: *The consistent information persists across the class of admissible repaired versions of the original instance.*

Of course, this approach has to be made precise, but it already suggests a paradigm shift, in the sense that we could decide to live with inconsistent data (or not to worry about certain ICs), the ICs are not constraints on the database states, but on the sets of answers to queries. Actually, they could be specified locally, with the query at hand. Even more, an *enhanced* SQL could provide such a construct.

In Example 2.3, we could think of posing the following query, enhanced with an additional clause specifying that we want the answers that are consistent with the FD:

SELECT *   (2.2)
FROM *Students*
WHERE *StuNum* > 100
CONSISTENT WITH *StuNum* -> *StuName*;

We would expect to obtain the answers (104, *claire stevens*) and (107, *pat norton*).

2.3   CHARACTERIZING CONSISTENT DATA

In order to define the admissible instances we mentioned above, we must first have a way to compare database instances, in terms of their distances to the instance D at hand.

Definition 2.4   Let D be a fixed instance for a relational schema $\mathcal{S}$.

(a) For two instances D_1, D_2 for $\mathcal{S}$, we say that D_1 *is at least as close to D as* D_2, denoted $D_1 \preceq_D D_2$, iff $\Delta(D, D_1) \subseteq \Delta(D, D_2)$. Here, $\Delta(S_1, S_2) := (S_1 \smallsetminus S_2) \cup (S_2 \smallsetminus S_1)$ is the symmetric set difference between two sets.

(b) $D_1 \prec_D D_2$ holds iff $D_1 \preceq_D D_2$, but not $D_2 \preceq_D D_1$.   ∎

This is one of the possible ways to compare database instances. It is the partial order used by Arenas et al. [1999]. It compares instances in terms of whole database tuples, i.e., ground atoms. The elements in $\Delta(D, D')$ can be seen as insertions and deletions of whole tuples into/from D, as we did in Example 2.3. We will consider alternative partial orders later on. Now, we are interested in the $\preceq_D$-minimal instances, those that are consistent and the closest to D.

Definition 2.5   [Arenas et al., 1999] Let D be an instance for schema $\mathcal{S}$, and IC a finite set of ICs, i.e., of sentences in $L(\mathcal{S})$.

(a) A *repair* of D is an instance D' for $\mathcal{S}$ that: 1. Satisfies IC, i.e., $D' \models IC$. 2. Is $\preceq_D$-minimal in the class of instances for $\mathcal{S}$ that satisfy IC.

(b) $Rep(D, IC)$ denotes the class of repairs of instance D wrt IC.   ∎

From this definition, we can see that a repair of D differs from D by a minimal set of insertions or deletions of tuples wrt set inclusion. Notice that the built-in predicates are not subject to changes, they have fixed extensions.

Example 2.6   Consider $D = \{P(a), P(b), Q(a), R(a), R(c)\}$, and $IC = \{\forall x(P(x) \rightarrow Q(x)), \forall x(Q(x) \rightarrow R(x))\}$.

In this case, $D \not\models IC$ since D does not contain $Q(b)$. We have two repairs for D:

(a) $D_1 = \{P(a), Q(a), R(a), R(c)\}$, for which $\Delta(D, D_1) = \{P(b)\}$; and

(b) $D_2 = \{P(a), P(b), Q(a), Q(b), R(a), R(b), R(c)\}$, for which $\Delta(D, D_2) = \{Q(b), R(b)\}$.

They are minimal, as expected, i.e., there is no consistent D' with: $\Delta(D, D') \subsetneq \Delta(D, D_1)$ or $\Delta(D, D') \subsetneq \Delta(D, D_2)$.

For example, $D_3 = \{P(a), P(b), Q(a), Q(b), R(a), R(b)\}$ is consistent, but is not a repair, because $\Delta(D, D_3) = \{Q(b), R(b), R(c)\}$, which properly contains $\Delta(D, D_2)$. ∎

Using this notion of repair, we can define the consistent information in a database as the information that is invariant under all possible repairs. This characterization can be applied in particular to query answers.

Definition 2.7   [Arenas et al., 1999] Consider an instance D of schema $\mathcal{S}$, a set IC of ICs, and an n-ary query $\mathcal{Q}(\bar{x})$ (defined) in $L(\mathcal{S})$:

(a) $\bar{t} \in \mathcal{U}^n$ is a *consistent answer* to $\mathcal{Q}(\bar{x})$ in D, denoted $D \models_{IC} \mathcal{Q}[\bar{t}]$, iff $D' \models \mathcal{Q}[\bar{t}]$ for every $D' \in Rep(D, IC)$;

(b) for a boolean query $\mathcal{Q}$, *yes* is the consistent answer, denoted $D \models_{IC} \mathcal{Q}$, iff $D' \models \mathcal{Q}$ for every $D' \in Rep(D, IC)$;

(c) $CQAS(D, IC, \mathcal{Q})$ denotes the set of consistent answers. ∎

According to this definition, $\bar{t}$ is a consistent answer from D when it is an answer to the same query from every possible repair of D.

Notice that a consistent answer is a so-called *certain answer* in the sense of Imielinski and Lipski [1984], who represent an *incomplete* database D as a set $\mathcal{I}$ of (regular) instances. The intended answers to a query posed to D are those that are certain in the sense that they can be obtained from each of the instances in $\mathcal{I}$.

Example 2.8   (Example 2.3 continued) In this case, we have the set $\{FD\}$ of ICs, where FD is the functional dependency: *Students* : $StuNum \rightarrow StuName$. For the query $\mathcal{Q}_1(x, y)$: $Students(x, y)$, it holds: $D \models_{\{FD\}} Students[104, claire\ stevens]$.

Similarly, $D \models_{\{FD\}} (Students(101, john\ bell) \vee Students(101, joe\ logan))$. Here we have a boolean query that is consistently true. We also have: $D \models_{\{FD\}} \exists x\, Students(101, x)$. However, $D \not\models_{\{FD\}} Students(101, john\ bell)$. ∎

Repairs can be seen as new instances obtained from D by means of virtual updates. By keeping the inconsistent data in the original instance, we retain information that is consistent, e.g., that student number 101 is associated to students *john bell* or *joe logan*, which would be lost if we decided to get rid of the tuples participating in a violation of an IC.

Notice that, according to the definition of repair (Definition 2.5), two repairs may differ in terms of the *number* of insertions or deletions of tuples, i.e., in terms of the cardinality of $\Delta(D, D')$. It is possible to consider an alternative *repair semantics* that is based on this cardinality consideration (cf. Section 2.5.5).

The notion of repair has helped us characterize the consistent data in a database. From this point of view, a repair can be considered as an auxiliary concept. If we want to compute consistent information, in particular consistent answers to queries, we may try to avoid explicitly computing and materializing repairs. As the following example shows, there may be too many of them.

Example 2.9   [Arenas et al., 2003b] The following instance is inconsistent wrt the FD $R : A \rightarrow B$.

R	A	B
	1	0
	1	1
	.	.
	n	0
	n	1

There are n pairs of tuples that, in combination, violate the FD. In this case, we have 2^n possible repairs, i.e., an exponential number in the size of the original instance.   ∎

2.4   WHAT DO WE DO THEN?

For the moment, and loosely speaking, (the problem of) *consistent query answering* (CQA) will refer to the problem of deciding if a tuple is a consistent answer to a query or to the problem of computing all the consistent answers to a query.

The simple Example 2.9 already shows that solving this problem by computing all the repairs of an inconsistent instance D, followed by querying them to detect what they have in common, should be avoided whenever possible. Alternative approaches have been investigated in the literature for CQA. Basically, they can be classified into two main categories.

1. *Query rewriting:* The basic idea is to take the original query, Q, the one expecting consistent answers, and try to transform it into a new query Q', such that the usual answers from D to Q' are exactly the consistent answers to Q from D. That is, we want:

$$D \models_{IC} Q[\bar{t}] \quad \text{iff} \quad D \models Q'[\bar{t}]. \tag{2.3}$$

Ideally, the query Q' should be easy to compute from Q and IC; and Q' should be easy to evaluate on D. For example, we would like to see the query (2.2) translated into a usual SQL query that can be evaluated directly on the given inconsistent instance.

The success of this endeavor will depend on all the parameters involved and their interaction: D, IC, and Q. In some cases this is possible (cf. Chapter 2). However, it might be the case that the rewriting Q' can only be achieved in a language that is more expressive than the one used for Q, and whose evaluation on a database has a higher complexity (than the one of evaluation of relational calculus queries) (cf. Chapters 4 and 5).

2. *Compact representation of repairs:* Instead of explicitly displaying all the possible repairs, we may attempt to represent them in compact terms, all at once. There are several alternatives in this direction, but they can be classified in their turn in two main different categories.

2.1. *Logical specification:* The repairs are *axiomatized* by means of a logical theory, i.e., they become the models of the latter. Reasoning about all repairs amounts to reasoning from the theory. Of course, different logical formalisms can be considered.

Notice that the definition of consistent answer is *model-theoretic*, in the sense that it appeals to a class of intended models; in this case, the one formed by the repairs of the original instance. In situations like this, it is common to try to provide a logical characterization of the class by means of a formal specification.

2.2. *Graph-theoretic representation:* The tuples in the original database become the vertices of a graph or an hypergraph. An edge corresponds to a violation of an IC by a combination of vertices; those are the vertices in (or connected by) the edge. Repairs appear as certain subsets of the graph, e.g., maximal independent sets. Algorithms for consistent query answering can be obtained as algorithms on graphs. Complexity results for consistent query answering can be obtained from complexity results for computational problems in graph theory.

Query rewriting and compact specifications of repairs are not necessarily mutually exclusive approaches. For example, using a logical specification can be seen as a form of query rewriting, if the theory itself is seen as a part of the new query. However, the resulting query can be quite complex. On the other side, it is possible to obtain query rewritings through graph-theoretic considerations and algorithms.

We will describe these approaches in subsequent chapters. Simple query rewriting in Section 3.1, graph- and hypergraph-theoretic representations in Section 3.3, and logical representations of repairs in Chapter 4.

2.5   SOME REPAIR SEMANTICS

The notion of repair in Definition 2.5 is based on two elements: (a) a class of database operations, namely insertions and deletions of full tuples; and (b) a particular partial order used to compare database instances wrt the given instance D, namely the one introduced in Definition 2.4. This is the notion of repair that was first investigated by Arenas et al. [1999], and will be one used in this work by default. However, other notions of repair have also been subsequently used and investigated in the literature, and we will occasionally refer to them.

Next, we introduce some alternative notions of repair, including as first item, and for future reference, also the one in Definition 2.5. Actually, all of them share the conditions in that definition, but the comparison partial order has to be changed depending on the kind of repair (condition (a2) in Definition 2.5). The minimality condition basically determines the kind of intended update operations.

2.5.1   TUPLE- AND SET-INCLUSION-BASED REPAIRS

Database operations are insertions and deletions of (full) database tuples. The partial order between instances is defined by: $D_1 \preceq_D D_2$ iff $\Delta(D_1, D) \subseteq \Delta(D_2, D)$. The corresponding class of repairs is denoted by $Rep^{ts}(D, IC)$ if we want to emphasize the difference with the other classes of repairs. Otherwise, we keep using the notation $Rep(D, IC)$ introduced in Definition 2.5.

2.5.2   TUPLE-DELETION- AND SET-INCLUSION-BASED REPAIRS

This is exactly as in Section 2.5.1, but only deletions of tuples are allowed as database operations. In this case, we still use the same partial order $\preceq_D$, but it can now be expressed as: $D_1 \preceq_D^d D_2$ iff $(D \smallsetminus D_1) \subseteq (D \smallsetminus D_2)$.[2] The class of repairs is denoted with $Rep^{ds}(D, IC)$. In Example 2.6, we have $D_1 \in Rep^{ds}(D, IC)$, but $D_2 \notin Rep^{ds}(D, IC)$.

Repairs in this class are the only ones in the class of tuple-oriented repairs that can be used to restore consistency wrt to denial constraints. However, we may decide to use only repairs of this kind to restore consistency wrt inclusion dependencies, in spite of the fact that they can also be enforced through tuple insertions (cf. Example 2.6). This is the repair semantics adopted and investigated by Chomicki and Marcinkowski [2005]. Under this repair semantics there is the basic assumption that the database instance at hand is *closed*, in the sense that no insertions of new tuples are accepted.

A good reason for adopting this kind of repair semantics in some cases is that, when the inclusion dependency has existentially quantified variables and we insert tuples to enforce them, we may have to invent data values for the inserted tuples. This is what the next repair semantics does (cf. also Section 4.1.4).

2.5.3   TUPLE-INSERTION- AND SET-INCLUSION-BASED REPAIRS

This repair semantics was studied by Calì et al. [2003] and considered only in the context of key constrains and inclusion dependencies (cf. Sections 5.3 and 5.5 for more details). The former are repaired through tuple deletions, and the latter, through tuple insertions. Except for this restriction, the definition of repair is as in Section 2.5.1. In Example 2.6, only D_2 could be a repair. This repair semantics is applied when the database at hand is considered to be incomplete and is then completed via additional tuple insertions.

If we denote the class of repairs with $Rep^{is}(D, IC)$, in Example 2.6 we have: $D_2 \in Rep^{is}(D, IC)$, but $D_1 \notin Rep^{is}(D, IC)$.

---

[2]If we wanted the partial order to capture the fact that only tuple deletions are allowed, we could add the extra condition that $(D_1 \smallsetminus D) = (D_2 \smallsetminus D) = \emptyset$. However, it is easier to specify first the kind of operations allowed, and then, on that basis, define the partial order.

As indicated above, an important issue is that, when the inclusion dependencies have existential quantifiers, then values have to be invented for them. Calì et al. [2003] chose those values arbitrarily from the underlying database domain $\mathcal{U}$.

Example 2.10   Consider the instance $D = \{P(a)\}$ and the IC: $\forall x(P(x) \rightarrow \exists y R(x, y))$. The repairs for this inconsistent instance are of the form: $D^u = \{P(a), R(a, u)\}$, where $u \in \mathcal{U}$. This leads to possibly infinitely many repairs.   ∎

Value inventions are in general non-deterministic, and complex to handle. Actually, they can lead to the undecidability of consistent query answering, i.e., of deciding if a tuple is a consistent answer to a query [Calì et al., 2003]. We explore these issues in more detail in Section 4.1.4 and Chapter 5.

2.5.4   NULL INSERTIONS-BASED REPAIRS

Under this repair semantics, existentially quantified inclusion dependencies are repaired by insertions of null values (cf. Section 4.1.5 for more details).

In Example 2.10, the only repair would be $D' = \{P(a), R(a, null)\}$. Bravo and Bertossi [2006] use a single null value for restoring consistency, and it behaves as an SQL NULL. This same repair semantics has been used in peer data exchange systems [Bertossi and Bravo, 2007]. Data are moved around at query answering time, and this process is driven by consistency restoration of inter-peer data exchange constraints.

Both *unknown* and *labeled nulls* (from a collection $\mathcal{N} = \{\lambda_1, \lambda_2, \ldots\}$) are used by Molinaro and Greco [2010] to restore consistency wrt a restricted class of FDs and referential ICs. The unknown values are used to represent the disjunctive information involved in violation of an FD, e.g., #1 for *john bell* $\vee$ *joe logan* associated to student number 101 in Example 2.3, and labeled nulls for value invention as required by referential ICs.

2.5.5   TUPLE- AND CARDINALITY-BASED REPAIRS

These are defined as in Section 2.5.1 (i.e., Definition 2.5), but with the partial order: $D_1 \preceq^c_D D_2$ iff $|\Delta(D_1, D)| \leq |\Delta(D_2, D)|$. Here, $|\cdot|$ is used to denote the cardinality of a set. The set of repairs of an instance D under this semantics is denoted by $Rep^{tc}(D, IC)$.

In Example 2.6, we have $D_1 \in Rep^{tc}(D, IC)$, but $D_2 \notin Rep^{tc}(D, IC)$. This repair semantics was briefly considered in Arenas et al. [2003a], and studied in more detail by Arieli et al. [2006], Lopatenko and Bertossi [2007] and Afrati and Kolaitis [2009]. It will be revisited in Section 5.7.

2.5.6   ATTRIBUTE-BASED REPAIRS

So far, we have considered repairs that insert or delete full tuples. Attribute-based repairs are obtained by changing attribute values in database tuples. Since this can be done in different ways and satisfying different criteria, we do not find a single attribute-based repair semantics. Different forms have been investigated in the literature [Bertossi et al., 2008, Bohannon et al., 2005, Flesca et al., 2010a, Franconi et al., 2001, Wijsen, 2005]. We now give an example that shows the idea, without committing to any specific attribute-based semantics.

Example 2.11 Consider $D = \{P(a_1, b_1), P(a_1, b_2)\}$, and the FD: $A \to B$, of the second attribute upon the first.

Candidates to be repairs could be, after eliminating duplicates if necessary, $D_1 = \{P(a_1, b_3)\}$, with $b_3 \in (\mathcal{U} \smallsetminus \{b_1, b_2\})$, or $D_2 = \{P(a_1, b_1), P(a_2, b_2)\}$, $D_3 = \{P(a_1, b_1)\}$ (by changing b_2 into b_1), etc. ∎

Possibly conditions on repairs could be, for example, minimizing the *number* of value changes [Flesca et al., 2010a, Franconi et al., 2001]. In the previous example, D_1 has 2, D_2 has 2, and D_3, has 1. However, if the values are numerical, we might want to consider some sort of aggregated distance between the old and the new values. This alternative is investigated by Bertossi et al. [2008] and Lopatenko and Bertossi [2007].

Changes of attribute values can be simulated via a combination of a deletion and an insertion of tuples. However, it is easy to see that a tuple-based repair semantics applied to this combination may not lead to a (minimal) attribute-based repair.

Finally, we should mention that null values can be used in attribute-based repairs too. This idea has been developed by Bertossi and Li [2011], in applications to privacy enforcement, where sensitive information is protected via null-based virtual updates of the views that specify the sensitive data.

Example 2.12 Consider the instance $D = \{P(a, b), R(b, c)\}$, and the denial constraint $\forall xyz \neg (P(x, y) \wedge R(y, z))$ that prohibits a join of P and R.

A natural null-based and also attribute-based repair could be $D_1 = \{P(a, null), R(null, c)\}$, but also $D_2 = \{P(a, null), R(b, c)\}$. In the case, of D_1 we would be assuming that *null* behaves as an SQL NULL, so that the prohibited join does not apply. ∎

2.5.7 PROJECT-JOIN REPAIRS

Wijsen [2006] considers a set of FDs on a universal relation. Under the most common repair semantics, violations of the FDs would be solved by tuple deletions (cf. Section 2.5.1). Having a universal relation, this kind of repair may lead to loss of useful information. A whole tuple could be deleted (in a repair) even if the FD violation is due to the misspelling of a value in a tuple. In this case, an attribute-based repair might be more natural. Actually, it is shown that attribute-based repairs of an instance D could be obtained via tuple deletions, but not from the original instance, but from a modified instance $\sigma(D)$.

Instance $\sigma(D)$ is an instance for the same schema as D, and is obtained by applying a *project-join dependency* σ that is entailed by (obtained from) the set Σ of FDs. A project-join dependency specifies a series of projections of a relation D on certain attributes and then the join of the resulting sub-relations [Abiteboul et al., 1995, Wijsen, 2006]. D satisfies σ iff $\sigma(D) = D$.

When D is inconsistent wrt the FDs Σ, it may hold that $\sigma(D)$ has extra tuples wrt D, and does not satisfy Σ either. Next, tuple-deletion-based repairs wrt Σ are applied to $\sigma(D)$, obtaining a class of repairs $Rep^s(\sigma(D), \Sigma)$ for D. Depending on the choice of σ, attribute-based repairs for D wrt Σ can be simulated via the repairs in $Rep^s(\sigma(D), \Sigma)$.

Example 2.13   [Wijsen, 2006] Consider the following universal relation with a set Σ of FDs:

D	Name	Birth	Sex	ZIP	City
	An	1964	F	7000	Mons
	Ed	1962	M	7000	Bergen

$Name \rightarrow \{Birth, Sex, ZIP\},$
$ZIP \rightarrow City.$

The second FD is violated, and there are two tuple-deletions-based repairs, each containing one of the two original tuples. Instead, generate the project-join dependency $\sigma = \bowtie$ [{$Name, Birth, Sex, ZIP$}, {$ZIP, City$}], and apply it to D, i.e., create two relations by projecting D on the two sets of attributes, obtaining

Name	Birth	Sex	ZIP
An	1964	F	7000
Ed	1962	M	7000

ZIP	City
7000	Mons
7000	Bergen

and join them next, obtaining the instance

$\sigma(D)$	Name	Birth	Sex	ZIP	City
	An	1964	F	7000	Mons
	Ed	1962	M	7000	Bergen
	An	1964	F	7000	Bergen
	Ed	1962	M	7000	Mons

The last two tuples have been inserted through the join. The resulting instance is still inconsistent wrt Σ. Now, applying tuple-based repairs to it we obtain two repairs for $\sigma(D)$, the so-called *project-join repairs* of D:

D_1	Name	Birth	Sex	ZIP	City
	An	1964	F	7000	Mons
	Ed	1962	M	7000	Mons

D_2	Name	Birth	Sex	ZIP	City
	An	1964	F	7000	Bergen
	Ed	1962	M	7000	Bergen

These repairs have on the original instance the same effect as attribute-based repairs that change the city values. ∎

It is also established by Wijsen [2006] that the repairs of D wrt Σ obtained via $\sigma(D)$ (i.e., first tuple insertions into D due to the application of σ followed by tuple deletions) lead to a version of consistent query answering that may have lower complexity than the one associated to the class of direct tuple-deletion-based repairs. Actually, there are cases where tractability of CQA based on project-join repairs can be achieved while tuple-based repairs applied directly to the original instance lead to an intractable CQA problem (cf. Chapter 5).

Some comparisons of different repair semantics can be found in [Lopatenko and Bertossi, 2007] and [Afrati and Kolaitis, 2009]. Unless we explicitly say otherwise, in the following and by default, we will always consider the repair semantics in Definition 2.5. However, all the semantics superficially described in this section will be revisited in Chapter 5.

CHAPTER 3

Tractable CQA and Query Rewriting

3.1 RESIDUE-BASED REWRITING

A first attempt to do query rewriting was proposed by Arenas et al. [1999]. The basic idea is to enforce ICs locally, at the level of database literals appearing in the query. This leads to a transformation of the original query, via a combination with the ICs. More precisely, given a query Q to be posed on the inconsistent instance D, and expecting consistent answers, Q is qualified with appropriate information derived from the interaction between Q and the set IC of ICs. The resulting query would be posed to, and answered from, the original instance D as usual. This would avoid the explicit computation of the repairs for D. This query rewriting approach is particularly appealing if the transformed query Q' is easy to produce and evaluate. Let us illustrate the idea by means of an example.

Example 3.1 Consider the instance $D = \{P(a), P(b), R(b), R(c)\}$, and the integrity constraint $\varphi : \forall x (P(x) \to R(x))$. The instance is inconsistent, because $R(a) \notin D$.

First, consider the query $Q_1(x) : R(x)$ about the tuples in the table for R. In this case, if a tuple belongs to R, say $R(d) \in D$, no violation can be produced wrt φ. So, we do not modify the atom in Q_1.

Now, consider the query $Q_2(x) : P(x)$ about the tuples in P. In this case, if a tuple belongs to P, say $P(d) \in D$, then that tuple is involved in a violation if $R(d) \notin D$. In consequence, for $P(d)$ to be a consistent answer, $R(d)$ should also be in D. Thus, we modify the query by adding this additional condition: $Q'_2(x) : P(x) \wedge R(x)$.

If we pose this query to D as usual, we obtain as set of answers: $\{\langle b \rangle)\}$, which coincides with the consistent answers according to Definition 2.7.

Finally, consider the query is $Q_3(x) : \neg R(x)$ (assuming, for illustration, that the database domain coincides with the active domain). In this case, for similar reasons, we modify the query as follows: $Q'_3(x) : \neg R(x) \wedge \neg P(x)$. If we pose it to D, we obtain: $\{\langle c \rangle)\}$, the same as with the model-theoretic definition.

In the last two queries above we have syntactically modified the original query. The atom in the query was appended a *residue* of its interaction with the IC. Actually, this residue and the interaction can be captured by means a a simple *resolution* step, i.e., by canceling complementary literals [Lloyd, 1987].

In the case of $\mathcal{Q}_2$, we have the formulas $P(x)$ and $\neg P(x) \vee R(x)$ (writing the IC in clausal form), which after one resolution step produce the appended residue $R(x)$. Similarly, with the query $\neg R(x)$, we obtain the residue $\neg P(x)$ that was appended to $\mathcal{Q}_3$.

Along the same line, for query $\mathcal{Q}_1$, we do not get any residue, and the query is not changed, as expected. In this case, the answers to $\mathcal{Q}_1$ are also the consistent answers to $\mathcal{Q}_1$.   ∎

As we can see from this example, the idea is to enforce the integrity constraints; and by doing so, discriminate between tuples in the answer set. This idea has been applied in *semantic query optimization*, where ICs, that embody semantic information, are used to optimize query answering. However, in that case, the assumption is that ICs are satisfied by the database [Chakravarthy et al., 1990]. Actually, the *residue of a literal L* wrt to an IC in clausal form $\psi : \forall \bar{x}(L_1 \vee \cdots \vee L_n)$ can always be obtained by means of a *resolution* step between L and ψ. This is shown more clearly in the next example.

Example 3.2   (Example 2.3 continued) The FD can be written in clausal form as follows:

$$FD : \forall x \forall y \forall z (\neg Students(x, y) \vee \neg Students(x, y) \vee y = z) .$$

Now, if the query is $\mathcal{Q}(x, y) : Students(x, y)$, we can apply resolution with the query atom and the first disjunct of FD, which are both eliminated because they are complementary literals. We obtain the *resolvent clause*: $\forall z(\neg Students(x, z) \vee y = z)$, and it is appended as a residue to the original query, obtaining the transformed query:

$$\mathcal{Q}'(x, y) := Students(x, y) \wedge \forall z(\neg Students(x, z) \vee y = z), \tag{3.1}$$

which is logically equivalent to the rewriting (1.3) shown in Chapter 1. The new query is asking about the student numbers, with their associated student names, that do not appear in the database with more than one student name. This query can be seen as obtained as the result of the application of a syntactic operator T, which takes the query and appends as conjuncts the residues of the literals in the query wrt to the ICs.

In this case, if we apply T again, to the database atoms in $\mathcal{Q}'$, we obtain a query that is logically equivalent to $\mathcal{Q}'$. That is, nothing essentially new is obtained.

If $\mathcal{Q}'$ is posed to the original database, we obtain the answers: (104, *claire stevens*) and (107, *pat norton*), which are exactly the consistent answers to the query. We do not obtain (101, *john bell*), nor (101, *joe logan*). They are filtered out by the residue.   ∎

In general, the transformation operator T, that was introduced by Arenas et al. [1999], is defined on queries that are conjunctions of literals and ICs that are universal, actually in clausal form. T has to be applied iteratively, as the following example shows.

Example 3.3   Consider a set of integrity constraints in clausal form (we omit the universal quantifiers), $IC: \{R(x) \vee \neg P(x) \vee \neg Q(x), \; P(x) \vee \neg Q(x)\}$, and the query about $Q(x)$.

A first application of operator T is obtained with one residue for each of the ICs:

$$T^1(Q(x)) := Q(x) \wedge (R(x) \vee \neg P(x)) \wedge P(x) .$$

Now, we apply T again, to the database literals in the appended residues:

$$\begin{aligned}
T^2(Q(x)) \quad &:= \quad Q(x) \wedge (T(R(x)) \vee T(\neg P(x))) \wedge T(P(x)). \\
&= \quad Q(x) \wedge (R(x) \vee (\neg P(x) \wedge \neg Q(x))) \wedge P(x) \wedge (R(x) \vee \neg Q(x)). \quad (3.2)
\end{aligned}$$

And again:

$$T^3(Q(x)) := Q(x) \wedge (R(x) \vee (\neg P(x) \wedge T(\neg Q(x)))) \wedge P(x) \wedge (T(R(x)) \vee T(\neg Q(x))) .$$

Since $T(\neg Q(x)) = \neg Q(x)$ and $T(R(x)) = R(x)$, we obtain: $T^3(Q(x)) = T^2(Q(x))$.

In order to obtain the consistent answers, we have to pose query (3.2) to the original instance.

■

In the previous examples we obtained a finite fixed point. Such a fixed point might not always exist. So, in general, the application of operator T will produce an *infinitary* query: $T^\omega(Q(\bar{x})) := \bigwedge_{n<\omega} T^n(Q(\bar{x}))$. This query has to be satisfied as a possibly infinite conjunction or an infinite theory in predicate logic. In the last example, we obtained that $T^\omega(Q(x))$ is (logically equivalent to) $T^1(Q(x)) \wedge T^2(Q(x))$.

Many questions naturally arise about the properties of this iterative process. Most prominently, about its correctness and finite termination. In the rest of this section we summarize some of the results reported by Arenas et al. [1999].

Depending on conditions satisfied by Q and IC, the operator T may be *sound* or *complete* (or both). These properties are stated as follows.

1. *Soundness*: Every tuple computed via T is consistent in the semantic sense, that is

$$D \models T^\omega(Q)[\bar{t}] \implies D \models_{IC} Q[\bar{t}] .$$

This means that the syntactic rewriting operator T eventually does not sanction as consistent an answer that is not consistent in the semantic sense.

2. *Completeness*: Every semantically consistent tuple can be obtained via T, that is

$$D \models_{IC} Q[\bar{t}] \implies D \models T^\omega(Q)[\bar{t}] .$$

This means that the operator T is powerful enough to eventually capture every semantically consistent answer to the query.

There are natural and useful syntactic classes of queries and ICs for which T has these properties. We mention some of them here.

For soundness, the following is a sufficient condition.

1. ICs are universal, i.e., logically equivalent to sentences in prenex normal form with only universal quantifiers. For example, functional dependencies, some inclusion dependencies without existential quantifiers, like $\forall x(P(x) \to Q(x)), \forall x \forall y(R(x, y) \to P(x))$.

As an additional requirement, we have:

   1.1. Universal queries, or

   1.2. Domain independent, but possibly non-universal queries, e.g., $\exists x P(x, y)$, $\exists x \forall y(R(x, y) \to S(x, y))$.

   In the case of queries of the form $\bar{Q}\chi$, with $\bar{Q}$ a prefix of quantifiers, and χ a quantifier-free formula in clausal form, the operator is first applied as follows: $T(\bar{Q}\chi) := \bar{Q}T(\chi)$ [Arenas et al., 1999].

For completeness, we have as sufficient condition:

2. The query is a conjunction of literals, and the set IC of ICs is such, that both 2.1. and 2.2. below hold:

   2.1. *Binary integrity constraints*, i.e., each of them is universal and mentions at most two database relations (plus possibly built-ins).

   2.2. *Generic integrity constraints*, i.e., that do not determine the truth of particular tuples. More precisely, for every ground tuple $P(\bar{t})$: $IC \not\models P(\bar{t})$ and $IC \not\models \neg P(\bar{t})$.

   For example, we can have the queries: $P(u, v)$, $R(u, v) \wedge \neg P(u, v)$; and $IC = \{\forall x \forall y(P(x, y) \to R(x, y)), \forall x \forall y \forall z(P(x, y) \wedge P(x, z) \to y = z)\}$.

The soundness and completeness properties are expressed in terms of the infinitary operator T^{ω}, and do not say anything about the possibility of obtaining a finite rewritten query as the result of applying T iteratively. This issue requires a separate analysis. As expected, finite termination may come in different forms.

1. *Syntactic termination*: In the iteration process to determine $T^{\omega}(Q)$ nothing syntactically new is obtained beyond some finite step. More precisely, $T^{\omega}(Q(\bar{x}))$ is *syntactically finite* if there is an $n \in \mathbb{N}$, such that $T^n(Q(\bar{x}))$ and $T^{n+1}(Q(\bar{x}))$ are syntactically the same.

2. *Semantic termination*: From some finite step on, only logically equivalent formulas to the previous ones are obtained. More precisely, $T^{\omega}(Q(\bar{x}))$ is *semantically finite* if there is an $n \in \mathbb{N}$, such that, for all $m \geq n$, $\forall \bar{x}(T^n(Q(\bar{x})) \equiv T^m(Q(\bar{x})))$ is logically valid.

3. *Instance-dependant semantic termination:* The first two alternatives are independent from the original database. It is possible to examine semantic termination wrt particular instances [Arenas et al., 1999].

In those favorable cases, if the finite termination point can be detected, the original first-order query $\mathcal{Q}$ can be translated into a first-order query, say $T^n(\mathcal{Q})$, like the one in (3.2), which, when posed and answered as usual to/from the original database D, will obtain the consistent answers to $\mathcal{Q}$ (assuming soundness and completeness). In these cases, consistent answer can be computed in polynomial time in the size of D, in *data complexity* (cf. Chapter 5 for complexity issues). Now we describe some results on finite termination obtained by Arenas et al. [1999].

There are necessary and sufficient conditions for *syntactic finite termination*. It holds for any kind of queries iff IC is universal and *acyclic*. That is, there is $f: \{P_1, \ldots, P_n, \neg P_1, \ldots, \neg P_n\} \to \mathbb{N}$, a *level mapping* on database "literal" predicates, such that, for every constraint in IC, say $\bar{\forall}(\bigvee_{i=1}^{k} L_i(\bar{x}_i) \vee \psi(\bar{x}))$, and every $1 \leq i, j \leq k$, if $i \neq j$, it holds $f(\neg L_i) > f(L_j)$.[1]

Intuitively, given an IC, $\bar{\forall}(L_1(\bar{x}_1) \vee \cdots \vee L_k(\bar{x}_k) \vee \psi(\bar{x}))$, if we want to obtain the consistent answers to $\neg L_i(\bar{x}_i)$, then all of $L_1(\bar{x}_1), \ldots, L_{i-1}(\bar{x}_{i-1}), L_{i+1}(\bar{x}_{i+1}), \ldots, L_k(\bar{x}_k), \psi(\bar{x})$ have to be evaluated; and we expect them to have a level lower than the one of $\neg L_i$.

Example 3.4 Consider the query $\mathcal{Q}(u, v): R(u, v) \wedge P(u, v)$, and $IC = \{\forall x \forall y (P(x, y) \to R(x, y)), \forall x \forall y \forall z (P(x, y) \wedge P(x, z) \to y = z)\}$.

To compute consistent answers (i.e., consistent tuples) for P, from the first IC we get residue R: It should be $f(P) > f(R)$. For P, from the second IC we get $\neg P$ as (a part of) the residue: It should be $f(P) > f(\neg P)$. To compute $\neg P$, we get no residue. To compute R, we get no residue either. Now, to compute $\neg R$, from the first IC we get residue $\neg P$: It should be $f(\neg R) > f(\neg P)$.

It is easy to see that the following level mapping satisfies de conditions: $f: P \mapsto 2, R \mapsto 1, \neg P \mapsto 1, \neg R \mapsto 2$. As a consequence, IC is acyclic. ∎

For example, sets of functional dependencies are always acyclic. However, with sets of inclusion dependencies, acyclicity may be lost. Checking acyclicity is clearly decidable.

For *semantic finite termination*, there are some sufficient conditions. For example, when queries are conjunctions of literals of the form $L_i(\bar{x})$, and, as an additional requirement, the set IC of universal ICs:

1. Contains only *uniform* constraints: In each constraint, each of the variables appearing in any of the literals also appears in some of the other literals in the same constraint; or

2. Is such that, for each literal L_i in a constraint, there is $n_i \in \mathbb{N}$, such that $\forall \bar{x}(T^{n_i}(L_i(\bar{x})) \to T^{n_i+1}(L_i(\bar{x})))$ is logically true.

Example 3.5 (a) Consider the set $IC = \{\forall xy(P(x, y) \to R(x, y)), \forall xy(R(x, y) \to P(x, y)), \forall xyz(P(x, y) \wedge P(x, z) \to y = z)\}$. These are all uniform constraints. For queries $\mathcal{Q}_1(u, v): P(u, v)$ and $\mathcal{Q}_2(u, v): R(u, v)$, it holds $T^2(\mathcal{Q}_i) \to T^3(\mathcal{Q}_i)$.

---

[1] $\bar{\forall}$ denotes the universal closure, i.e., a prefix of universal quantifiers that universally closes the formula that follows, producing a sentence.

(b) For the multi-valued dependency, $\bar{\forall}(P(x, y, z) \wedge P(x, u, v) \rightarrow P(x, y, v))$ (it is not uniform, but condition 2. right above holds), and the query $\mathcal{Q}(x, y, z) : P(x, y, z)$, it holds $T^3(\mathcal{Q}) \rightarrow T^4(\mathcal{Q})$. ∎

The residue-based query rewriting approach to CQA was slightly extended and sharpened by Celle and Bertossi [2000]. The algorithm, *QUECA*, inspired by the T operator, syntactically terminates for *binary* ICs, i.e., universal and containing at most two database literals plus built-ins. This class includes FDs, non-existentially quantified inclusion dependencies, range constraints, etc. *QUECA* is based on a careful syntactical analysis and memorization of residues and subsumption relationships between them. It was implemented on *XSB* [Sagonas et al., 1994], whose "tabling" techniques were used to avoid redundant computation of residues. It also offered interaction with DBMSs; in this case, IBM DB2.

3.2   EXTENDING QUERY REWRITING

The first-order query rewriting approach to CQA based on the T operator has some clear limitations. The most obvious one is that it works properly for a limited class of queries and ICs. The former are basically restricted to conjunctions of literals; and the latter, to universal ICs. And even in those cases, we may obtain an infinitary query. As a consequence, this technique is applied to universal queries and constraints, and not to other common cases of queries and constraints, e.g., referential ICs or conjunctive queries with projection. However, it is clear that, in principle, there could be alternative approaches to CQA via FO query rewriting, at least for some other cases of queries and ICs.

Example 3.6   (Example 3.2 continued) The query $\mathcal{Q}_1(x) : \exists y\, Students(x, y)$ has a simple, actually trivial, FO rewriting, namely $\mathcal{Q}'_1(x) : \exists y\, Students(x, y)$. If $\mathcal{Q}'_1$ is posed to the inconsistent databases as usual, we will obtain exactly the consistent answers to $\mathcal{Q}_1$.

Now, the query $\mathcal{Q}_2(y) : \exists x\, Students(x, y)$ also has a FO rewriting; in this case, $\mathcal{Q}'_2(y) : \exists x(Students(x, y) \wedge \forall z(\neg Students(x, z) \vee y = z))$, which can be obtained by existentially quantifying over x the query in (3.1). ∎

This example shows that there are quite intuitive and correct FO rewritings for other combinations of queries and ICs that are not necessarily based on the T operator. This problem is retaken in Section 3.4.

The main advantages of FO query rewriting are: (a) it can be directly implemented on top of relational DBMS, using SQL queries; and (b) it provides a polynomial time mechanism for computing consistent answers. Not surprisingly, much effort has been dedicated to find both FO rewriting methods and/or polynomial time algorithms for CQA. In fact, this problem has been investigated in the literature for certain classes of conjunctive queries (and unions thereof) and denial constraints, mainly key constraints [Chomicki and Marcinkowski, 2005, Fuxman and Miller,

2007, Grieco et al., 2005, Wijsen, 2009a,b]. In the rest of this section we show some of the results that have been obtained.

We conclude this section by pointing out that FO query rewriting has some intrinsic limitations (which apply in particular to the T operator as a mechanism for producing FO query rewritings). They come from the fact that, for some classes of queries and constraints, there is provably no FO rewriting, no matter what method we apply. This is due to expressibility and complexity properties of the CQA problem that are addressed in Chapter 5.

3.3   GRAPHS, HYPERGRAPHS AND REPAIRS

Arenas et al. [2001, 2003b] proposed a graph-theoretic representation of all the tuple-based repairs of an inconsistent instance. It was used for deriving some polynomial-time algorithms for CQA, and also analyzing its computational complexity. The queries were simple *aggregate queries*, and the ICs, only functional dependencies (cf. Section 5.6). Since then, the methodology has been extended and applied in other situations [Chomicki and Marcinkowski, 2005], including other repair semantics [Bertossi et al., 2008, Lopatenko and Bertossi, 2007] (cf. Chapter 5).

Example 3.7   Consider the schema $R(A, B)$ with the following set FD of FDs $A \rightarrow B$ and $B \rightarrow A$. The following instance $D = \{R(a_1, b_1), R(a_1, b_2), R(a_2, b_2), R(a_2, b_1)\}$ is inconsistent.

The repairs of D can be represented by means of an undirected graph, as follows: 1. Each database atom of D is a vertex. 2. There is an edge between two atoms iff they jointly violate one of the FDs. We obtain the following *conflict graph* $\mathcal{G}(D, FD)$:

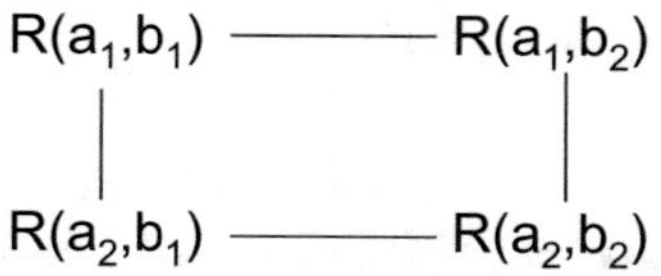

$$R(a_1,b_1) \text{————} R(a_1,b_2)$$
$$| \qquad\qquad\qquad |$$
$$R(a_2,b_1) \text{————} R(a_2,b_2)$$

Figure 3.1: Conflict-Graph $\mathcal{G}(D, FD)$.

Here, the repairs of D are: $D_1 = \{R(a_1, b_1), R(a_2, b_2)\}$ and $D_2 = \{R(a_1, b_2), R(a_2, b_1)\}$. We can see that each repair of D corresponds to a *maximal independent set* in $\mathcal{G}(D, FD)$, and vice versa. Dually, there is a one-to-one correspondence between the repairs and the *maximal cliques* in the *complement graph* of $\mathcal{G}(D, \{FD\})$, which is obtained by dropping the original edges, and creating new edges between vertices not originally connected.   ∎

For FO queries, the first systematic investigation of graph-theoretic methods for CQA was undertaken by Chomicki and Marcinkowski [2005]. They focused on denial constraints, FDs in particular, and some extensions with inclusion dependencies. Denial constraint violations can be solved only by tuple deletions, but inclusion dependency violations by both tuple deletions and insertions. However, Chomicki and Marcinkowski [2005] consider only tuple deletions for inclusion dependencies. With denial constraints we may have to generate an hypergraph instead of a graph.

Example 3.8 Consider the denial constraint, $\delta: \forall xyz\neg(P(x,y) \wedge P(x,z) \wedge R(y,z))$, and the inconsistent instance $D = \{P(a,b), P(a,c), P(e,f), R(b,c), R(e,f)\}$. Since three tuples simultaneously participate in the violation of δ, we obtain a hyperedge connecting three vertices. The following is the *conflict hypergraph* $\mathcal{HG}(D, \{\delta\})$:

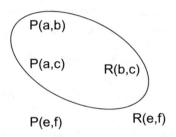

Figure 3.2: Conflict-Hypergraph $\mathcal{HG}(D, IC)$.

Now, a *maximal independent set* of $\mathcal{HG}(D, \{\delta\})$ is a $\subseteq$-maximal set of vertices that does not contain a hyperedge. As with FDs, there is a one-to-one correspondence between maximal independent sets and repairs of D. In this case, we have the following repairs: $D_1 = \{P(a,c), P(e,f), R(b,c), R(e,f)\}$, $D_2 = \{P(a,b), P(e,f), R(b,c), R(e,f)\}$, $D_3 = \{P(a,b), P(a,c), P(e,f), R(e,f)\}$. ∎

Conflict graphs and hyper-graphs provide a compact, implicit representation of all the repairs of an instance wrt a set of denial cosntraints. Graph-theoretic concepts, algorithms, and results can be used then for CQA, obtaining rewriting or polynomial time algorithms for query answering in tractable cases, and also for identifying cases of higher complexity. Actually, some cases of schemas with denial constraints (including key constraints and FDs) were identified for which CQA for certain simple classes of conjunctive queries is tractable [Chomicki and Marcinkowski, 2005], and polynomial time algorithms were developed [Chomicki et al., 2004].

Also, tractable cases and hard cases that include inclusion dependencies in addition to denial constraints have been found. Inclusion dependencies are not (equivalent to) denial constraints, but they can be treated like them if only tuple deletions are allowed to restore consistency [Chomicki and Marcinkowski, 2005]. The hypergraph-based methodology has also been extended and applied to general universal constraints, of which denial constraints form a subclass [Staworko and Chomicki, 2010] (cf. Section 5.3).

3.4 KEYS, TREES, FORESTS AND ROOTS

The complexity analysis of CQA for key constraints and conjunctive queries with projection, that was started by Chomicki and Marcinkowski [2005], was extended by Fuxman and Miller [2005, 2007], where a broader tractable class was identified and characterized, and polynomial time algorithms were presented. Actually, the syntactic class $\mathcal{C}_{Tree}$ of conjunctive queries was identified for which CQA is still tractable [Fuxman and Miller, 2005]. The class is defined in graph-theoretic terms, but this time, on the basis of the syntactic structure of the query and its interaction with the key dependencies.

More precisely, the *join graph* $\mathcal{G}(\mathcal{Q})$ of a boolean conjunctive query $\mathcal{Q}$ is a directed graph, whose vertices are the database atoms in $\mathcal{Q}$ [Fuxman and Miller, 2005]. There is an arc from L to L' if $L \neq L'$ and there is a variable w that occurs at the position of a non-key attribute in L that also occurs in L'. Furthermore, there is a self-loop at L if there is a variable that occurs at the position of a non-key attribute in L, and at least twice in L.

By definition, a query $\mathcal{Q}$ belongs to the class $\mathcal{C}_{Tree}$ if $\mathcal{Q}$ does not have repeated relations symbols, $\mathcal{G}(\mathcal{Q})$ is a forest, and every non-key to key join of $\mathcal{Q}$ is full i.e., involves the whole key. Open conjunctive queries can be accommodated in this class by treating the free variables in them as constants in the definition of their join graph [Wijsen, 2009b].

Example 3.9 Consider the following boolean queries, where the primary keys of the relations involved are underlined and all the variables are existentially quantified: $\mathcal{Q}_1 : \bar{\exists}(P(\underline{x}, y) \wedge R(\underline{y}, w) \wedge T(\underline{u}, \underline{v}, y))$; $\mathcal{Q}_2 : \bar{\exists}T(\underline{x}, \underline{y}, y)$; $\mathcal{Q}_3 : \bar{\exists}(R(\underline{x}, y) \wedge P(\underline{y}, z) \wedge S(\underline{z}, \underline{u}))$; and $\mathcal{Q}_4 : \bar{\exists}(R(\underline{x}, y) \wedge S(\underline{w}, z) \wedge P(\underline{y}, u))$. The four respective associated join graphs are shown in Figure 3.3.

$\mathcal{G}(\mathcal{Q}_1)$ and $\mathcal{G}(\mathcal{Q}_2)$ are not forests, therefore their queries are not in $\mathcal{C}_{Tree}$. Even though $\mathcal{G}(\mathcal{Q}_3)$ is a forest, since it has a non-key to key join that is not full, it does not belong to $\mathcal{C}_{Tree}$. $\mathcal{Q}_4$ is in $\mathcal{C}_{Tree}$ because $\mathcal{G}(\mathcal{Q}_3)$ is a forest and all the non-key to key joins are full. ∎

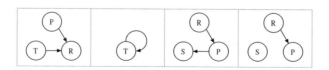

Figure 3.3: Join-Graphs for Queries $\mathcal{Q}_1$, $\mathcal{Q}_2$, $\mathcal{Q}_3$, $\mathcal{Q}_4$.

The class $\mathcal{C}_{Tree}$ was slightly reformulated and extended, to the class $\mathcal{C}_{Forest}$ [Fuxman and Miller, 2007], that in essence contains queries $\mathcal{Q}$ that are sets of queries in $\mathcal{C}_{Tree}$, the set of the connected components of $\mathcal{Q}$. CQA becomes tractable for queries in $\mathcal{C}_{Forest}$, and, even more, CQA can be done by means of FO query rewriting algorithms [Fuxman and Miller, 2007].

Actually, for every query Q in $\mathcal{C}_{Forest}$, there is a FO rewriting Q' for CQA. For example, the boolean query

$$Q : \exists x \exists y \exists z (R(\underline{x}, z) \wedge S(\underline{z}, y))$$

belongs to $\mathcal{C}_{Tree}$, and has the following consistent rewriting [Fuxman and Miller, 2007]:

$$Q' : \exists x \exists z' (R(\underline{x}, z') \wedge \forall z (R(\underline{x}, z) \rightarrow \exists y S(\underline{z}, y))) .$$

Query Q' is a *consistent rewriting* of Q in the sense that it is a FO query and:

$$D \models_{KC} Q \quad \text{iff} \quad D \models Q' .$$

Notice that Q' is a first-order boolean non-conjunctive query, but by being FO, it still can be evaluated in polynomial time (in the size of the database).

The class $\mathcal{C}_{Forest}$ is rather sharp, in the sense that not satisfying some of their syntactic conditions increases complexity [Fuxman and Miller, 2007].[2] Implementation of these rewriting algorithms for the class $\mathcal{C}_{Tree}$, and experimentation with them, are reported in [Fuxman et al., 2005]. Tractable classes of unions of queries in $\mathcal{C}_{Tree}$ are identified by Grieco et al. [2005].

The class of *key-rooted* conjunctive queries, denoted $\mathcal{C}_{Rooted}$, was introduced by Wijsen [2009b]. So as the class $\mathcal{C}_{Forest}$, it is also relative to key constraints. However, the class appeals to the *join graph* of the query [Beeri et al., 1983] (as opposed to the Fuxman-Miller graphs $\mathcal{G}(Q)$ above), and is defined in semantic terms. This semantic characterization allows all its members to have simple consistent (FO) rewritings, which makes their consistent answering tractable. Unfortunately, and in contrast with $\mathcal{C}_{Forest}$, there is no (known) syntactic characterization of $\mathcal{C}_{Rooted}$, nor a known procedure for deciding membership for a conjunctive query of $\mathcal{C}_{Rooted}$.

However, there is a syntactic subclass of $\mathcal{C}_{Rooted}$, and then a sufficient syntactic condition for membership of $\mathcal{C}_{Rooted}$, that allows to prove that $\mathcal{C}_{Rooted}$ contains $\mathcal{C}_{Tree}$ [Wijsen, 2009b]. Actually, the inclusion is proper since queries in $\mathcal{C}_{Rooted}$ may contain self-joins, i.e., repeated predicates, and may also be cyclic in the sense of Beeri et al. [1983]. Whereas the conditions on queries in the definition of $\mathcal{C}_{Tree}$ imply their acyclicity (in same sense) [Wijsen, 2009b, Cor. 5]. This result can be extended, establishing that $\mathcal{C}_{Rooted}$ also contains $\mathcal{C}_{Forest}$, whose queries may contain cycles.

The classes of conjunctive queries (and unions thereof) that admit a consistent rewriting and have been described or mentioned above contain many cases of queries that are common in database practice. Systems based on FO query rewriting have been implemented [Celle and Bertossi, 2000, Chomicki et al., 2004, Fuxman et al., 2005]. However, for complexity-theoretic or expressivity reasons, FO query rewriting cannot be applied to all conjunctive queries (cf. Chapter 5). It is bound to having a limited applicability.

---

[2] Assuming that *NP* is different from *coNP*. In the rest of this work, whenever we make a loose claim about an increment of complexity, we are assuming that the usual and corresponding complexity-theoretic conjectures are true.

CHAPTER 4

Logically Specifying Repairs

We have seen that FO query rewriting approaches to CQA seem to work only for certain classes of first-order ICs and queries. Actually, as we will see in Chapter 5, a rewriting-based approach may have to appeal to logical languages that are more expressive than FO logic. Furthermore, our definition of repairs (and of consistent answers based on them) is not a logical specification. We provided a *model-theoretic* definition of consistent answers, i.e., that is defined wrt to a set of intended models (the repairs).

Under these circumstances, it is natural to ask if it is possible to logically specify the class of repairs, i.e., as the set of models of a logical specification, say $Spec(Rep(D, IC))$. Having $Spec(Rep(D, IC))$, we could think of obtaining logical consequences or doing reasoning from $Spec(Rep(D, IC))$. In particular, for consistent answers $\bar{t}$ to queries $\mathcal{Q}(\bar{x})$, the following should hold:

$$D \models_{IC} \mathcal{Q}[\bar{t}] \iff Spec(Rep(D, IC)) \models_{\mathcal{L}} \mathcal{Q}[\bar{t}], \tag{4.1}$$

where $\models_{\mathcal{L}}$ stands for a logical-consequence relation that is suitable for the logic, say $\mathcal{L}$, of *Spec*. On the right-hand side of (4.1), $\mathcal{Q}[\bar{t}]$ can be understood as the formula defining the query with its free variables replaced by the corresponding constants in $\bar{t}$.

In some cases, on the right-hand side of (4.1) we may have to replace $\mathcal{Q}$ by a slightly, cosmetically modified version, say $\mathcal{Q}'$, to adapt the query to the formalism of the specification. (We do not consider this to be a real, essential rewriting of $\mathcal{Q}$ as described and needed in previous sections. Cf. Example 4.3 below.)

We could also think of deriving algorithms for consistent query answering from the logical entailment relation on the right-hand side of (4.1). The possibility of doing so largely depends on the kind of specification and logic involved in it. In this direction, the first remark we have to make is that CQA is *non-monotonic*, as the following example shows.

Example 4.1 Consider the database instance D below, and FD: *Name* $\rightarrow$ *Salary*.

Employee	Name	Salary
	page	5000
	smith	3000
	stowe	7000

In this case, we have
$$D \models_{\{FD\}} Employee(page, 5000).$$
However,
$$D \cup \{Employee(page, 8000)\} \not\models_{\{FD\}}$$
$$Employee(page, 5000).$$

We can see that, when we increase the instance by adding a new tuple, we lose one of the consistent answers. ∎

In some cases, as we will see below, it is possible to isolate D from $Spec(Rep(D, IC))$, and replace (4.1) by

$$D \models_{IC} \mathcal{Q}(\bar{t}) \iff D \cup \Phi \models_{\mathcal{L}} \mathcal{Q}(\bar{t}), \tag{4.2}$$

where D if the original database instance, or more precisely, a logical representation of it, e.g., the finite conjunction of its database atoms. In this case, the "combination" of Φ and $\mathcal{Q}$ can be seen as a form of rewriting of $\mathcal{Q}$ for obtaining the consistent answers to $\mathcal{Q}$. Of course, the rewriting could be much more intricate that those considered in Chapter 3, in a logic that is much more complex or expressive than FO predicate logic. We will see examples of this below.

Different kinds of non-monotonic specifications have been explored in the literature. In the following sections we summarize and briefly describe some of them. Three logical characterizations that we do not present are: (a) repairs as branches of *non-monotonic analytic tableaux* [Bertossi and Schwind, 2004]; (b) repairs as models of *disjunctive databases* [Molinaro et al., 2009]; and (c) repairs as models of *signed theories* [Arieli et al., 2006].

4.1 SPECIFYING REPAIRS WITH LOGIC PROGRAMS

In this section we will concentrate mainly on universal ICs. See Sections 4.1.4 and 4.1.5 for extensions to existential ICs, like referential ICs.

Given an instance D, and a set IC of universal ICs, the collection, $Rep(D, IC)$ (cf. Definition 2.5), of all database repairs of D wrt IC can be represented in a compact form, as the class of intended models of a *disjunctive logic program*, $\Pi(D, IC)$. The semantics of such a program is the *disjunctive stable model semantics* [Gelfond and Lifschitz, 1990, 1991] (cf. also [Baral, 2003, Gelfond and Leone, 2002] for more recent introductions to the subject). In consequence, the repairs correspond to the stable models of this *repair program*. Before presenting the repair programs, we give a short introduction to logic programs with stable model semantics.

4.1.1 DISJUNCTIVE DATALOG WITH STABLE MODEL SEMANTICS

We consider disjunctive Datalog programs Π [Eiter et al., 1997, Gelfond and Lifschitz, 1991] with a finite number of rules of the form

$$A_1 \vee \ldots \vee A_n \leftarrow P_1, \ldots, P_m, \; not \; N_1, \ldots, \; not \; N_k, \tag{4.3}$$

with $0 \leq n, m, k$, and the A_i, P_j, N_s are positive first-order atoms. The terms in these atoms are constants or variables. The variables in the A_i, N_s appear all among those in the P_j. The constants in program Π form the (finite) Herbrand universe U of the program. The ground version of program Π, $gr(\Pi)$, is obtained by instantiating the variables in Π in all possible combinations using values from U. The Herbrand base HB of Π consists of all the possible atomic sentences obtained by instantiating the predicates in Π in U.

A subset M of HB is a model of Π if it satisfies $gr(\Pi)$, that is: For every ground rule $A_1 \vee \ldots \vee A_n \leftarrow P_1, \ldots, P_m$, $not\ N_1, \ldots,\ not\ N_k$ of $gr(\Pi)$, if $\{P_1, \ldots, P_m\} \subseteq M$ and $\{N_1, \ldots, N_k\} \cap M = \emptyset$, then $\{A_1, \ldots, A_n\} \cap M \neq \emptyset$. M is a minimal model of Π if it is a model of Π, and Π has no model that is properly contained in M. $MM(\Pi)$ denotes the class of minimal models of Π.

Now, take $S \subseteq HB(\Pi)$, and transform $gr(\Pi)$ into a new, positive program $gr(\Pi) \downarrow$ (i.e., without not), as follows: Delete every rule $A_1 \vee \ldots \vee A_n \leftarrow P_1, \ldots, P_m$, $not\ N_1, \ldots,\ not\ N_k$ for which $\{N_1, \ldots, N_k\} \cap S \neq \emptyset$. Next, transform each remaining rule $A_1 \vee \ldots \vee A_n \leftarrow P_1, \ldots, P_m$, $not\ N_1, \ldots,\ not\ N_k$ into $A_1 \vee \ldots \vee A_n \leftarrow P_1, \ldots, P_m$. Now, S is a *stable model* of Π if $S \in MM(gr(\Pi) \downarrow)$. It can be proved that a stable model of Π is indeed a model, and also a minimal one.

It can be proved that disjunctive Datalog programs with stable model semantics generalize Datalog and Datalog$^{s\neg}$, i.e., Datalog extended with stratified negation [Abiteboul et al., 1995, Ceri et al., 1989]. Datalog and Datalog$^{s\neg}$ programs have a single (intended) model that can be computed in a bottom-up manner starting from the extensional database (EDB), i.e., the set of *facts* or rules of the form (4.3) with $n = 1, m = k = 0$, and A_1 ground. This only model coincides with the single stable model that is obtained when the stable model semantics is applied to Datalog and Datalog$^{s\neg}$ programs. In general, disjunctive Datalog programs and non-disjunctive programs (i.e., $n = 1$ in (4.3)) with non-stratified negation may have multiple stable models.

That with disjunctive Datalog we do have an extension of both Datalog and Datalog$^{s\neg}$ is indicated by the (probable) difference in computational complexity. The problem of deciding if a ground atom A is entailed by a disjunctive Datalog program Π, i.e., A is true in all the stable models of Π, is Π_2^P-complete in the size of the EDB. The same problem can be solved in polynomial time for Datalog and Datalog$^{s\neg}$ programs. (cf. [Dantsin et al., 2001] for more details.) The additional expressive power of disjunctive Datalog programs comes handy for applications to database repairs and CQA (cf. Chapter 5).

4.1.2   REPAIR PROGRAMS

First and independent approaches to the specification of repairs with logic programs are due to Arenas et al. [2003a] and Greco et al. [2003]. They use the stable model semantics. Here we present, by means of a hopefully sufficiently generic example, the simpler and more general approach introduced by Barceló and Bertossi [2003], that has been later extended, refined, and optimized [Barceló et al., 2003, Bravo and Bertossi, 2006, Caniupan and Bertossi, 2010].

The program $\Pi(D, IC)$ uses annotation constants in an extra attribute in the database predicates. The idea of introducing this kind of annotations was inspired by an earlier specification of repairs as minimal models of a theory written in annotated predicate logic [Arenas et al., 2000] (cf. Section 4.2).

The annotations and their intended semantics can be found in the following table. The intended semantics will be formally captured, as expected, by their use and specification in the logic programs.

Annotation	Atom	The atom $P(\bar{a})$ is...
$\mathbf{t_a}$	$P(\bar{a}, \mathbf{t_a})$	advised to be made true (inserted)
$\mathbf{f_a}$	$P(\bar{a}, \mathbf{f_a})$	advised to be made false (deleted)
$\mathbf{t^\star}$	$P(\bar{a}, \mathbf{t^\star})$	true or becomes true
$\mathbf{t^{\star\star}}$	$P(\bar{a}, \mathbf{t^{\star\star}})$	it is true in the repair

We will illustrate this approach to CQA by means of examples.

Example 4.2   Consider the instance $= \{S(a), S(b), Q(b)\}$, and $IC \colon \forall x (S(x) \to Q(x))$.
The repair program $\Pi(D, IC)$ contains the following rules and facts.

1. The program facts are the original database tuples: $S(a)$, $S(b)$, $Q(b)$.

2. Annotation rules capture part of the intended meaning of annotations (similarly for predicate Q):

$$S\_(x, \mathbf{t^\star}) \leftarrow S(x).$$
$$S\_(x, \mathbf{t^\star}) \leftarrow S\_(x, \mathbf{t_a}).$$

They say that whatever was in the initial instance or was inserted afterwards becomes annotated with $\mathbf{t^\star}$. They are necessary when there are several, possibly interacting ICs, and the repair process may have to go through several steps. We use a new predicate of the form $P\_$ associated to each original predicate P, because the former has an extra argument, for the annotations.

3. The most important rules are the *repair rules*, those associated to the ICs:

$$S\_(x, \mathbf{f_a}) \vee Q\_(x, \mathbf{t_a}) \quad \leftarrow \quad S\_(x, \mathbf{t^\star}), \; not \; Q(x).$$
$$S\_(x, \mathbf{f_a}) \vee Q\_(x, \mathbf{t_a}) \quad \leftarrow \quad S\_(x, \mathbf{t^\star}), \; Q\_(x, \mathbf{f_a}).$$

The bodies of the rules capture a violation of the IC. i.e., a tuple in S that is not in Q. The heads propose alternative ways to restore consistency by means of tuple insertions or deletions, in this case, deletions from S or insertions in Q. In general, there will be one repair rule per ICs (in some cases, like referential ICs we may have to add an auxiliary rule (cf. Section 4.1.4.1).

4. Interpretation rules, that have to do with the semantics of annotations (similarly for predicate Q):

$$S\_(x, \mathbf{t^{\star\star}}) \leftarrow S\_(x, \mathbf{t^\star}), \; not \; S\_(x, \mathbf{f_a}).$$

They are used to collect at the end, when the process has stabilized, the atoms (annotated with $\mathbf{t^{\star\star}}$) that will form a repair. Those are the tuples that were originally in the database or were inserted, but never deleted.

5. Program constraints:

$$\leftarrow \; S\_(x, \mathbf{t_a}), S\_(x, \mathbf{f_a}).$$
$$\leftarrow \; Q\_(x, \mathbf{t_a}), Q\_(x, \mathbf{f_a}).$$

They are used to filter out the models of the program where the combinations expressed as conjunctions in the bodies become true. In this case, models where a same tuple is both inserted and deleted.

The stable models of the program $\Pi(D, IC)$ are:

$$\mathcal{M}_1 \;=\; \{S(a), S(b), Q(b), S\_(a, \mathbf{t}^\star), S\_(b, \mathbf{t}^\star), Q\_(b, \mathbf{t}^\star), Q\_(a, \mathbf{t_a}), S\_(a, \mathbf{t}^{\star\star}),$$
$$S\_(b, \mathbf{t}^{\star\star}), Q\_(b, \mathbf{t}^{\star\star}), Q\_(a, \mathbf{t}^\star), Q\_(a, \mathbf{t}^{\star\star})\}, \;\; \text{and}$$

$$\mathcal{M}_2 \;=\; \{S(a), S(b), Q(b), S\_(a, \mathbf{t}^\star), S\_(b, \mathbf{t}^\star), Q\_(b, \mathbf{t}^\star), S\_(a, \mathbf{f_a}), S\_(b, \mathbf{t}^{\star\star}),$$
$$Q\_(b, \mathbf{t}^{\star\star})\}.$$

The database repairs are in one-to-one correspondence with the stable models, and are obtained from the latter by selecting the atoms with annotation $\mathbf{t}^{\star\star}$. They are:

$$D_1 = \{S(a), S(b), Q(b), Q(a)\}, \;\; \text{and} \;\; D_2 = \{S(b), Q(b)\}. \qquad \blacksquare$$

Since we are interested in consistent answers, and they have to be true in all the repairs, we can query the program under the *skeptical or cautious* semantics that sanctions as true wrt the program all what is true in all its stable models.

Example 4.3   (Example 4.2 continued) Consider the query $\mathcal{Q}(x)\colon S(x)$, asking for the consistent tuples in table S. We introduce a new predicate, *Ans*, to collect the answers, and the original query is transformed into a simple query program $\Pi(\mathcal{Q})$, containing a single rule: $Ans(x) \leftarrow S(x, \mathbf{t}^{\star\star})$.

The stable models of the combined program $\Pi(D, IC) \cup \Pi(\mathcal{Q})$ are extensions of the stables models of $\Pi(D, IC)$, namely: $\mathcal{M}'_1 = \mathcal{M}_1 \cup \{Ans(a), Ans(b)\}$ and $\mathcal{M}'_2 = \mathcal{M}_2 \cup \{Ans(b)\}$. This sanctions $\langle b \rangle$ as the only consistent answer to the query, because $Ans(b)$ is the only answer atom that is true in all models. $\blacksquare$

Here, we have explicitly shown the stable models and their extensions. However, the evaluation of the program can be done by means of more focalized and optimized computational mechanisms. Systems for logic program evaluation under the stable model semantics provide some built-in optimizations. In CQA, the *DLV* system [Leone et al., 2006] has been successfully used for experimentation and implementing other systems on top of it [Arenas et al., 2003a, Caniupan and Bertossi, 2010, Eiter et al., 2008].

This logic programming approach to CQA has several advantages, among them:

(a) We can use a single and same repair program for all the queries expecting consistent answers. All we have to do is replace the query program on top of the repair program.

For example, in order to request the consistent answers to the query $\exists y P(x, y)$, the query program becomes $Ans(x) \leftarrow P(x, y, \mathbf{t}^{\star\star})$. Similarly, for the query $P(x, y) \wedge \neg Q(x, y)$, the query program is $Ans(x, y) \leftarrow P(x, y, \mathbf{t}^{\star\star})$, *not* $Q(x, y, \mathbf{t}^{\star\star})$.

(b) Queries are quite general. They can go beyond FO predicate logic, e.g., queries written in Datalog or Datalog$^{s\neg}$. If we are interested only FO queries, there is a general mechanism, the Lloyd-Topor transformation, to generate a query program from a FO query [Lloyd, 1987].

(c) Systems like *DLV* avoid explicitly computing all the stable models if possible, and offer several optimization techniques. They also offer connectivity to comercial DBMSs.

(d) Additional optimization techniques for query evaluation can be applied [Caniupan and Bertossi, 2010, Eiter et al., 2008], e.g., magic sets (cf. Section 4.1.3).

(e) The methodology is general enough to be applied to arbitrary FO queries and ICs, including among the latter, referential ICs (cf. Section 4.1.4).

(f) The semantics of disjunctive logic programs under stable model semantics takes care of our needs in CQA, e.g., the closed-world-assumption of databases; and also the minimality of repair actions. This is due to the minimality property of stable models and the "exclusive" interpretation of disjunctions in the rule heads.

Among possible drawbacks of the use of logic programs for CQA, we find efficiency. As we will discuss in Chapter 5, the repair programs provide the right level of complexity or expressive power needed for CQA. However, they cannot compete with FO query rewriting mechanisms when they exists and are available.

Notice that CQA based on repair programs follow under the patterns in (4.1) or (4.2). More precisely, we have:

$$D \models_{IC} \mathcal{Q}(\bar{t}) \iff \Pi(D, IC) \cup \Pi(\mathcal{Q}) \models_{sk} Ans(\bar{t}), \qquad (4.4)$$

where, on the right-hand side, the initial instance D is included in the program as a set of facts, and $\models_{sk}$ denotes *skeptical entailment* from the logic program (as being true in all stable models). In this case, the original query is represented by the combination of $\Pi(\mathcal{Q})$ and the query atom $Ans(\bar{x})$.

4.1.3   MAGIC SETS FOR REPAIR PROGRAMS

Naively applying the logic programming approach to CQA can be quite inefficient. Whenever optimization techniques are available, they should be applied.

A classic technique for optimizing query evaluation over Datalog programs (and extensions with limited use of negation) is the *magic sets method* (cf. [Ceri et al., 1989] for a good account of the classic methodology). The basic idea is to simulate (or capture certain aspects of) the top-down query evaluation approaches by means of bottom-up evaluation.

Bottom-up query evaluation methodologies are more appropriate for database applications because, by moving the data from the EDB upwards through the rules, all the answers to the query are simultaneously computed. However, possibly much redundant and useless data is propagated to the top. On the other side, top-down evaluation usually gets one answer at a time, but is much more sensitive to the query at hand, including the presence specific predicates and parameters. Taking them into account from the very beginning avoids the consideration of useless data in the computation process. As a consequence, the magic sets method is a bottom-up query evaluation methodology over Datalog programs that is more sensitive to the predicates and parameters in the query. This makes it more efficient than naive bottom-up evaluation.

As we indicated before (c.f. Section 4.1.1), Datalog programs (with or without stratified negation) have a single (stable) model that can be computed bottom-up, whereas disjunctive Datalog programs and non-disjunctive Datalog programs with non-stratified negation, as those that we need for our applications in CQA, require much more involved model generation mechanisms [Calimeri et al., 2006]. In consequence, the extension of classical magic sets methods to this kind of programs is not straightforward. Having them in order to make query evaluation more sensitive to the query at hand, for example, avoiding the computation of the extensions of useless predicates in the stable models, looks particularly appealing and useful.

Fortunately, the classic *magic sets method* for query evaluation in deductive databases has been recently extended to logic programs with stable model semantics [Cumbo et al., 2004, Faber et al., 2007]. They have been slightly adapted for applications to CQA [Caniupan and Bertossi, 2010]. The basic idea is to make query evaluation more efficient by using relevant information in the query, like constants and predicates, to guide the evaluation process. By doing so, only the relevant portion of the logic program and the relevant underlying data are used. Impressive improvements in performance for CQA based on repair programs are reported by Caniupan and Bertossi [2010]. We illustrate the approach by means of an example, to convey just the gist of the methodology, that, in our view, should become increasingly relevant for applications of the newer extensions of Datalog to data management.

Example 4.4   Consider $D = \{S(a), T(a)\}$, $IC = \{\forall x(S(x) \rightarrow Q(x)), \forall x(Q(x) \rightarrow R(x)), \forall x(T(x) \rightarrow W(x))\}$, and the query (program): $Ans(x) \leftarrow \underline{S}(x, \mathbf{t^{\star\star}})$. The combined program $\Pi(D, IC) \cup \Pi(Q)$ consists of the following rules:

1. $S(a)$. $T(a)$.
2. $\underline{S}(x, \mathbf{f_a}) \vee \underline{Q}(x, \mathbf{t_a}) \leftarrow \underline{S}(x, \mathbf{t^{\star}}), Q(x, \mathbf{f_a})$,
3. $\underline{S}(x, \mathbf{f_a}) \vee \underline{Q}(x, \mathbf{t_a}) \leftarrow \underline{S}(x, \mathbf{t^{\star}}),$ *not* $Q(x)$,
4. $\underline{Q}(x, \mathbf{f_a}) \vee \underline{R}(x, \mathbf{t_a}) \leftarrow \underline{Q}(x, \mathbf{t^{\star}}), R(x, \mathbf{f_a})$,
5. $\underline{Q}(x, \mathbf{f_a}) \vee \underline{R}(x, \mathbf{t_a}) \leftarrow \underline{Q}(x, \mathbf{t^{\star}}),$ *not* $R(x)$,
6. $\underline{T}(x, \mathbf{f_a}) \vee \underline{W}(x, \mathbf{t_a}) \leftarrow \underline{T}(x, \mathbf{t^{\star}}), W(x, \mathbf{f_a})$,
7. $\underline{T}(x, \mathbf{f_a}) \vee \underline{W}(x, \mathbf{t_a}) \leftarrow \underline{T}(x, \mathbf{t^{\star}}),$ *not* $W(x)$,
8. $\underline{S}(x, \mathbf{t^{\star}}) \leftarrow \underline{S}(x, \mathbf{t_a})$.
9. $\underline{S}(x, \mathbf{t^{\star}}) \leftarrow S(x)$.
10. $\underline{Q}(x, \mathbf{t^{\star}}) \leftarrow \underline{Q}(x, \mathbf{t_a})$.
11. $\underline{Q}(x, \mathbf{t^{\star}}) \leftarrow Q(x)$.
12. $\underline{R}(x, \mathbf{t^{\star}}) \leftarrow \underline{R}(x, \mathbf{t_a})$.
13. $\underline{R}(x, \mathbf{t^{\star}}) \leftarrow R(x)$.
14. $\underline{T}(x, \mathbf{t^{\star}}) \leftarrow \underline{T}(x, \mathbf{t_a})$.
15. $\underline{T}(x, \mathbf{t^{\star}}) \leftarrow T(x)$.
16. $\underline{W}(x, \mathbf{t^{\star}}) \leftarrow \underline{W}(x, \mathbf{t_a})$.
17. $\underline{W}(x, \mathbf{t^{\star}}) \leftarrow W(x)$.
18. $\underline{S}(x, \mathbf{t^{\star\star}}) \leftarrow \underline{S}(x, \mathbf{t^{\star}}),$ *not* $\underline{S}(x, \mathbf{f_a})$.
19. $\underline{Q}(x, \mathbf{t^{\star\star}}) \leftarrow \underline{Q}(x, \mathbf{t^{\star}}),$ *not* $\underline{Q}(x, \mathbf{f_a})$.
20. $\underline{R}(x, \mathbf{t^{\star\star}}) \leftarrow \underline{R}(x, \mathbf{t^{\star}}),$ *not* $\underline{R}(x, \mathbf{f_a})$.
21. $\underline{T}(x, \mathbf{t^{\star\star}}) \leftarrow \underline{T}(x, \mathbf{t^{\star}}),$ *not* $\underline{T}(x, \mathbf{f_a})$.
22. $\underline{W}(x, \mathbf{t^{\star\star}}) \leftarrow \underline{W}(x, \mathbf{t^{\star}}),$ *not* $\underline{W}(x, \mathbf{f_a})$.
23. $\leftarrow \underline{Q}(x, \mathbf{t_a}), \underline{Q}(x, \mathbf{f_a})$.
24. $Ans(x) \leftarrow \underline{S}(x, \mathbf{t^{\star\star}})$.

Its stable models are:

$$\mathcal{M}_1 = \{T(a), S(a), \underline{T}(a, \mathbf{t}^\star), \underline{S}(a, \mathbf{t}^\star), \underline{Q}(a, \mathbf{t_a}), \underline{S}(a, \mathbf{t}^{\star\star}), \underline{Q}(a, \mathbf{t}^\star), \underline{R}(a, \mathbf{t_a}), \underline{Q}(a, \mathbf{t}^{\star\star}),$$
$$\underline{R}(a, \mathbf{t}^\star), \underline{R}(a, \mathbf{t}^{\star\star}), Ans(a), \underline{W}(a, \mathbf{t_a}), \underline{T}(a, \mathbf{t}^{\star\star}), \underline{W}(a, \mathbf{t}^\star), \underline{W}(a, \mathbf{t}^{\star\star})\}.$$

$$\mathcal{M}_2 = \{T(a), S(a), \underline{T}(a, \mathbf{t}^\star), \underline{S}(a, \mathbf{t}^\star), \underline{Q}(a, \mathbf{t_a}), \underline{S}(a, \mathbf{t}^{\star\star}), \underline{Q}(a, \mathbf{t}^\star), \underline{R}(a, \mathbf{t_a}), \underline{Q}(a, \mathbf{t}^{\star\star}),$$
$$\underline{R}(a, \mathbf{t}^\star), \underline{R}(a, \mathbf{t}^{\star\star}), Ans(a), \underline{T}(a, \mathbf{f_a})\}.$$

$$\mathcal{M}_3 = \{T(a), S(a), \underline{T}(a, \mathbf{t}^\star), \underline{S}(a, \mathbf{t}^\star), \underline{S}(a, \mathbf{f_a}), \underline{W}(a, \mathbf{t_a}), \underline{T}(a, \mathbf{t}^{\star\star}), \underline{W}(a, \mathbf{t}^\star), \underline{W}(a, \mathbf{t}^{\star\star})\}.$$

$$\mathcal{M}_4 = \{T(a), S(a), \underline{T}(a, \mathbf{t}^\star), \underline{S}(a, \mathbf{t}^\star), \underline{S}(a, \mathbf{f_a}), \underline{T}(a, \mathbf{f_a})\}.$$

They indicate that there are no consistent answers to the query (there are no *Ans*-atoms in common). We can also see that the stable models represent repairs that also consider the last element of *IC*, that is not related to the query. The magic sets method transforms the repair program $\Pi(D, IC)$ into one that is relevant to the query at hand. In this case, the resulting *magic program* contains the following rules:[1]

1. *Magic rules*:

$magic\_S\_^{fb}(\mathbf{t}^{\star\star}) \leftarrow magic\_ans^f.$ $magic\_Q\_^{fb}(\mathbf{t_a}) \leftarrow magic\_S\_^{fb}(\mathbf{f_a}).$

$magic\_S\_^{fb}(\mathbf{t}^\star) \leftarrow magic\_S\_^{fb}(\mathbf{f_a}).$ $magic\_Q\_^{fb}(\mathbf{f_a}) \leftarrow magic\_S\_^{fb}(\mathbf{f_a}).$

$magic\_S\_^{fb}(\mathbf{f_a}) \leftarrow magic\_Q\_^{fb}(\mathbf{t_a}).$ $magic\_S\_^{fb}(\mathbf{t}^\star) \leftarrow magic\_Q\_^{fb}(\mathbf{t_a}).$

$magic\_Q\_^{fb}(\mathbf{f_a}) \leftarrow magic\_Q\_^{fb}(\mathbf{t_a}).$ $magic\_S\_^{fb}(\mathbf{t_a}) \leftarrow magic\_S\_^{fb}(\mathbf{t}^\star).$

$magic\_Q\_^{fb}(\mathbf{t_a}) \leftarrow magic\_Q\_^{fb}(\mathbf{t}^\star).$ $magic\_S\_^{fb}(\mathbf{t}^\star) \leftarrow magic\_S\_^{fb}(\mathbf{t}^{\star\star}).$

$magic\_S\_^{fb}(\mathbf{f_a}) \leftarrow magic\_S\_^{fb}(\mathbf{t}^{\star\star}).$ $magic\_Q\_^{fb}(\mathbf{t}^\star) \leftarrow magic\_Q\_^{fb}(\mathbf{t}^{\star\star}).$

$magic\_Q\_^{fb}(\mathbf{f_a}) \leftarrow magic\_Q\_^{fb}(\mathbf{t}^{\star\star}).$ $magic\_R\_^{fb}(\mathbf{t_a}) \leftarrow magic\_Q\_^{fb}(\mathbf{f_a}).$

$magic\_Q\_^{fb}(\mathbf{t}^\star) \leftarrow magic\_Q\_^{fb}(\mathbf{f_a}).$ $magic\_R\_^{fb}(\mathbf{f_a}) \leftarrow magic\_Q\_^{fb}(\mathbf{f_a}).$

$magic\_Q\_^{fb}(\mathbf{f_a}) \leftarrow magic\_R\_^{fb}(\mathbf{t_a}).$ $magic\_Q\_^{fb}(\mathbf{t}^\star) \leftarrow magic\_R\_^{fb}(\mathbf{t_a}).$

$magic\_R\_^{fb}(\mathbf{f_a}) \leftarrow magic\_R\_^{fb}(\mathbf{t_a}).$ $magic\_R\_^{fb}(\mathbf{t_a}) \leftarrow magic\_R\_^{fb}(\mathbf{t}^\star).$

$magic\_R\_^{fb}(\mathbf{t}^\star) \leftarrow magic\_R\_^{fb}(\mathbf{t}^{\star\star}).$ $magic\_R\_^{fb}(\mathbf{f_a}) \leftarrow magic\_R\_^{fb}(\mathbf{t}^{\star\star}).$

2. *Modified program rules*:

$Ans(x) \leftarrow magic\_Ans^f, \underline{S}(x, \mathbf{t}^{\star\star}).$

$\underline{S}(x, \mathbf{f_a}) \vee \underline{Q}(x, \mathbf{t_a}) \leftarrow magic\_S\_^{fb}(\mathbf{f_a}), magic\_Q\_^{fb}(\mathbf{t_a}), \underline{S}(x, \mathbf{t}^\star), \underline{Q}(x, \mathbf{f_a}).$

$\underline{S}(x, \mathbf{f_a}) \vee \underline{Q}(x, \mathbf{t_a}) \leftarrow magic\_S\_^{fb}(\mathbf{f_a}), magic\_Q\_^{fb}(\mathbf{t_a}), \underline{S}(x, \mathbf{t}^\star), not\ Q(x).$

$\underline{Q}(x, \mathbf{f_a}) \vee \underline{R}(x, \mathbf{t_a}) \leftarrow magic\_Q\_^{fb}(\mathbf{f_a}), magic\_R\_^{fb}(\mathbf{t_a}), \underline{Q}(x, \mathbf{t}^\star), \underline{R}(x, \mathbf{f_a}).$

$\underline{Q}(x, \mathbf{f_a}) \vee \underline{R}(x, \mathbf{t_a}) \leftarrow magic\_Q\_^{fb}(\mathbf{f_a}), magic\_R\_^{fb}(\mathbf{t_a}), \underline{Q}(x, \mathbf{t}^\star), not\ R(x).$

$\underline{S}(x, \mathbf{t}^\star) \leftarrow magic\_S\_^{fb}(\mathbf{t}^\star), \underline{S}(x, \mathbf{t_a}).$

$\underline{S}(x, \mathbf{t}^\star) \leftarrow magic\_S\_^{fb}(\mathbf{t}^\star), S(x).$

$\underline{Q}(x, \mathbf{t}^\star) \leftarrow magic\_Q\_^{fb}(\mathbf{t}^\star), \underline{Q}(x, \mathbf{t_a}).$

$\underline{Q}(x, \mathbf{t}^\star) \leftarrow magic\_Q\_^{fb}(\mathbf{t}^\star), Q(x).$

$\underline{R}(x, \mathbf{t}^\star) \leftarrow magic\_R\_^{fb}(\mathbf{t}^\star), \underline{R}(x, \mathbf{t_a}).$

$\underline{R}(x, \mathbf{t}^\star) \leftarrow magic\_R\_^{fb}(\mathbf{t}^\star), R(x).$

$\underline{S}(x, \mathbf{t}^{\star\star}) \leftarrow magic\_S\_^{fb}(\mathbf{t}^{\star\star}), \underline{S}(x, \mathbf{t}^\star), not\ \underline{S}(x, \mathbf{f_a}).$

---

[1]A general algorithm can be applied to do this transformation [Caniupan and Bertossi, 2010].

$Q_{-}(x, \mathbf{t}^{\star\star}) \leftarrow magic\_Q_{-}^{fb}(\mathbf{t}^{\star\star}), Q_{-}(x, \mathbf{t}^{\star}), not\ Q_{-}(x, \mathbf{f_a}).$
$R_{-}(x, \mathbf{t}^{\star\star}) \leftarrow magic\_R_{-}^{fb}(\mathbf{t}^{\star\star}), R_{-}(x, \mathbf{t}^{\star}), not\ R_{-}(x, \mathbf{f_a}).$

3. *Program denial*: $\leftarrow Q_{-}(x, \mathbf{t_a}), Q_{-}(x, \mathbf{f_a}).$

4. *Program facts*: $magic\_Ans^f, S(a), T(a).$

The modified program will never use rules associated to predicates T or W. Their initial extensions can also de ignored. Actually, the two stable models of the new program are:

$$
\begin{aligned}
\mathcal{M}_1 \ = \ & \{magic\_Ans^f, S(a), T(a), S_{-}(a, \mathbf{t}^{\star}), magic\_S_{-}^{fb}(\mathbf{t}^{\star\star}), magic\_S_{-}^{fb}(\mathbf{f_a}), magic\_S_{-}^{fb}(\mathbf{t_a}), \\
& magic\_S_{-}^{fb}(\mathbf{t}^{\star}), magic\_Q_{-}^{fb}(\mathbf{f_a}), magic\_Q_{-}^{fb}(\mathbf{t_a}), magic\_Q_{-}^{fb}(\mathbf{t}^{\star}), magic\_R_{-}^{fb}(\mathbf{f_a}), \\
& magic\_R_{-}^{fb}(\mathbf{t_a}), Q_{-}(a, \mathbf{t_a}), S_{-}(a, \mathbf{t}^{\star\star}), Q_{-}(a, \mathbf{t}^{\star}), R_{-}(a, \mathbf{t_a}), Ans(a)\}.
\end{aligned}
$$

$$
\begin{aligned}
\mathcal{M}_2 \ = \ & \{magic\_Ans^f, S(a), T(a), S_{-}(a, \mathbf{t}^{\star}), magic\_S_{-}^{fb}(\mathbf{t}^{\star\star}), magic\_S_{-}^{fb}(\mathbf{f_a}), magic\_S_{-}^{fb}(\mathbf{t_a}), \\
& magic\_S_{-}^{fb}(\mathbf{t}^{\star}), magic\_Q_{-}^{fb}(\mathbf{f_a}), magic\_Q_{-}^{fb}(\mathbf{t_a}), magic\_Q_{-}^{fb}(\mathbf{t}^{\star}), magic\_R_{-}^{fb}(\mathbf{f_a}), \\
& magic\_R_{-}^{fb}(\mathbf{t_a}), S_{-}(a, \mathbf{f_a})\}.
\end{aligned}
$$

As expected, we obtain the same empty set of consistent answers. The new program, although it looks more complex, can be evaluated much faster than the original one.   ∎

4.1.4   LOGIC PROGRAMS AND REFERENTIAL ICS

Until now, we haven't considered logic programs for referential ICs, or, more generally, existential ICs. The main reason is that before developing repair programs for them, we have to agree on a repair semantics for them. As discussed in Section 2.5, there are some alternatives. We illustrate them and their treatment with repair programs by means of an example.

Example 4.5   Consider $IC = \{\forall x (T(x) \rightarrow \exists y P(y, x))\}$ and the inconsistent instance $D = \{P(a, b), T(c), T(e), P(e, e)\}.$ ∎

4.1.4.1   Tuple deletions

According to the tuple-deletion repair semantics (cf. Section 2.5.2), there is only one repair for the instance in Example 4.5: $D' = \{P(a, b), T(e), P(e, e)\}$. The main rules for a repair program that captures this repair semantics are:

$$
\begin{aligned}
T_{-}(x, \mathbf{f_a}) \ &\leftarrow \ T_{-}(x, \mathbf{t}^{\star}),\ not\ aux(x). \\
aux(x) \ &\leftarrow \ P_{-}(x, y, \mathbf{t}^{\star}).
\end{aligned}
$$

4.1.4.2 Tuple insertions

For the inconsistency shown in Example 4.5, if we use the tuple-insertion repair semantics (cf. Section 2.5.3), we have as many repairs as elements in the underlying database domain. These repairs are of the form: $D^u = \{P(a, b), T(c), T(e), P(e, e), P(u, c)\}$, where $u \in \mathcal{U}$ is an arbitrary element.

If we assume that the domain is finite or finitely axiomatized via a predicate, *dom*, we can have a repair program for this semantics, with the following repair rule:

$$P\_(y, x, \mathbf{t_a}) \quad \leftarrow \quad T\_(x, \mathbf{t^\star}), \ not \ aux(x), dom(y), choice((x), y).$$
$$aux(x) \quad \leftarrow \quad P\_(x, y, \mathbf{t^\star}).$$

In this case, we are using the *non-deterministic choice operator* [Giannotti et al., 1997]. Here, *choice*$((x), y)$ chooses a single value for y from *dom* for each value of x that satisfies the first conditions in the rule body. That value for y is used to insert the tuple $P(y, x)$. The choice operator can always be eliminated, obtaining a standard logic program with stable model semantics. However, the choice operator makes the representations more compact and intuitive.

4.1.4.3 Tuple-insertions and deletions

Finally, if we adopt the original repair semantics in Definition 2.5, we may insert or delete tuples. In this case, for Example 4.5, we can combine the two previous approaches by considering a disjunctive rule:

$$P\_(y, x, \mathbf{t_a}) \vee T\_(x, \mathbf{f_a}) \quad \leftarrow \quad T\_(x, \mathbf{t^\star}), \ not \ aux(x), dom(y), choice((x), y).$$
$$aux(x) \quad \leftarrow \quad P\_(x, y, \mathbf{t^\star}).$$

In this case, we obtain the repairs: $D' = \{P(a, b), T(e), P(e, e)\}$ and $D^u = \{P(a, b), T(c), T(e), P(e, e), P(u, c)\}$, with $u \in \mathcal{U}$.

In the next section, we considered an alternative repair semantics for the case of existential ICs.

4.1.5   NULL-BASED TUPLE INSERTIONS

It is also possible to restore consistency of referential ICs by introducing null values. This requires making some preliminary decisions, most prominently, about the kind of null values and the repair semantics. The latter has to be modified in order to prefer the introduction of null values over arbitrary constants from the database domain. Another issue is that introducing null values, and even having them in the instance from the start, requires clarifying IC satisfaction in databases with null values. Satisfaction, or more precisely, violations, have to be captured in the bodies of repair rules. Also, the update operations (in the heads) depend on the semantics of null values and IC satisfaction.

A *null-based repair semantics* was presented and analyzed by Bravo and Bertossi [2006], and further studied and applied by Bertossi and Bravo [2007]. It is still tuple-based, but whenever existential ICs have to be repaired via a tuple insertion, a null value is used for the existentially quantified variable. Actually, a single null value is used, as in SQL databases. Bravo and Bertossi [2006] logically reconstructed the semantics of IC satisfaction and query answering *à la* SQL. We illustrate this approach with a new example.

Example 4.6 Consider the referential IC $\forall x \forall y (Course(x, y) \rightarrow \exists z \, Student(x, z))$; and the instance:

D	Course	StdID	Code
		21	null
		34	comp1805

Student	StdID	Name
	21	ann
	45	paul

There are two repairs under this null-based repair semantics:

D_1	Course	StdID	Code
		21	null

Student	StdID	Name
	21	ann
	45	paul

D_2	Course	StdID	Code
		21	null
		34	comp1805

Student	StdID	Name
	21	ann
	45	paul
	34	null

With this repair semantics we have a finite number of repairs, and we are also close to the database practice of inserting nulls to enforce referential ICs. ∎

Definition 4.7 Let D be a database instance, possibly containing *null*, and *IC* a set of universal and referential ICs. A repair D' of D wrt *IC* is an instance with the following properties.

(a) It has the same schema as D.

(b) It is consistent wrt *IC* (for a null-based notion of IC satisfaction [Bravo and Bertossi, 2006]).

(c) It is $\preceq_D^n$-minimal. ∎

The partial order $\preceq_D^n$ has to be defined in such a way that it privileges inserted tuples that contain *null* instead of other values from the database domain.

Definition 4.8 Let D be a fixed instance of a schema $\mathcal{S}$ whose universe $\mathcal{U}$ contains *null*. For D_1, D_2 instances for $\mathcal{S}$, $D_1 \preceq_D^n D_2$ iff:

(a) for every atom $P(\bar{t}) \in \Delta(D, D_1)$, with *null* $\notin \bar{t}$, it holds $P(\bar{a}) \in \Delta(D, D_2)$; and

(b) for every atom $P(\bar{t}_1, null, \ldots, \bar{t}_2, null, \ldots, \bar{t}_m) \in \Delta(D, D_1)$, with *null* $\notin \bar{t}_1, \ldots, \bar{t}_m$, it holds $P(\bar{t}_1, b_1, \ldots, \bar{t}_2, b_2, \ldots, \bar{t}_m) \in \Delta(D, D_2)$ with $b_1, b_2, \ldots \in \mathcal{U}$. ∎

Example 4.9   (Example 4.6 continued) For the exhibited repairs, it holds: $\Delta(D, D_1) =$ $\{Course(34, comp1805)\}$, $\Delta(D, D_2) = \{Student(34, null)\}$.

Consider the following repair candidate (it satisfies the referential IC):

D_3	Course	StdID	Code
		21	null
		34	comp1805

Student	StdID	Name
	21	ann
	45	paul
	34	tom

Now, $\Delta(D, D_3) = \{Student(34, tom)\}$, and then $D_2 \preceq^n_D D_3$, with $D_3 \not\preceq^n_D D_2$. As a consequence, D_3 is not $\preceq^n_D$-minimal. Thus, D_3 is not a repair.   ■

This repair semantics involves a notion of IC satisfaction that we haven't developed here. Details can be found in [Bravo and Bertossi, 2006]. It appeals to the notion of *relevant attributes* in an IC, as those for whom the occurrence of nulls is relevant for its satisfaction. Taking those relevant attributes into account avoids propagation of insertions of null values, even in the case of cycles in the set of referential ICs. As a consequence, this repair semantics produces only a finite number of (finite) repairs for each finite set of ICs that are universal of referential [Bravo and Bertossi, 2006]. Actually, checking if a tuple is a consistent answer under this semantics becomes decidable. This has to be contrasted with the unrestricted insertion of tuples, as in Section 4.1.4, that, when there are cycles in *IC*, can produce infinitely many repairs, actually of infinite size, and leads to the undecidability of consistent query answering [Cali et al., 2003] (cf. Sections 5.3 and 5.5).

The repair semantics presented in this section can also be captured by means of logic programs [Bertossi and Bravo, 2007, Bravo and Bertossi, 2006], and the magic sets method can be applied to them [Caniupan and Bertossi, 2010].

Example 4.10   (Example 4.5 continued) According to the new repair semantics, the violations of the referential IC can be repaired via a tuple deletion or a tuple insertion with null. This is captured by means of the repair rule:

$$P\_(null, x, \mathbf{t_a}) \vee T\_(x, \mathbf{f_a}) \quad \leftarrow \quad T\_(x, \mathbf{t}^\star), \; not \; aux(x), \; x \neq null.$$
$$aux(x) \quad \leftarrow \quad P\_(x, y, \mathbf{t}^\star), \; x \neq null, \; y \neq null.$$

The built-ins added to the rule bodies are related to the values for the relevant attributes in the constraint.   ■

Notice that in this section we have been still comparing database instances through set inclusion, via the symmetric difference of two sets of whole database tuples. In consequence, the repairs, in spite of the introduction of null values, are still tuple-oriented. A repair semantics based on changes of attribute values into *null* has been used in privacy enforcement and investigated in that context [Bertossi and Li, 2011]. Corresponding repair programs have been proposed.

4.2   REPAIRS IN ANNOTATED PREDICATE LOGIC

The theory in first-order predicate logic obtained by combining the database D (or its logical reconstruction [Reiter, 1984]) with the set IC of ICs is logically inconsistent if the former does not satisfy the latter. Using a different logic, we can consistently combine these two elements, and obtain a logical specification of the database repairs. Arenas et al. [2000] accomplish this by means of *annotated predicate calculus* (APC) [Kifer and Lozinskii, 1992], which assumes the existence of an underlying lattice of truth values. They are used to annotate atoms at the object level. Most typically, and beyond classical logic, those values are $\mathbf{t}, \mathbf{f}, \top, \bot$, for *true, false, contradictory,* and *unknown,* respectively, with $\bot < \mathbf{t}, \mathbf{f} < \top$.

The database atoms in an APC-theory could be annotated with classical truth values, e.g., *Employee(smith,* 3000)$: \mathbf{t}$, *Employee(smith, x)*$: \mathbf{f}$, *Employee(smith, y)*$: \top$. However, in order to embed both D and IC into a single, useful and consistent APC-theory, we have to make some considerations: (a) ICs are hard, not to be given up, but the database atoms are flexible, subject to repairs. (b) In case of a conflict between a constraint and the database instance, the advise is to change the truth value of the database atoms to the value prescribed by the constraint.

This requires a more complex annotation lattice, *Lat,* to be used as follows: 1. For database atoms: $\mathbf{t_d}, \mathbf{f_d}$. 2. For constraint atoms: $\mathbf{t_c}, \mathbf{f_c}$. 3. For advisory values: $\mathbf{t_a}, \mathbf{f_a}$. The latter are used to advise the resolution of conflicts between $\mathbf{d}$-values and $\mathbf{c}$-values by favoring $\mathbf{c}$-values. All this is captured by means of the lattice *Lat* shown in Figure 4.1.

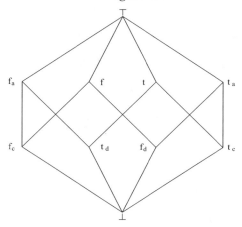

Figure 4.1: The annotation lattice *Lat.*

In *Lat,* it holds: (a) For every $\mathbf{s} \in Lat$, $\bot \leq \mathbf{s} \leq \top$, and (b) $lub(\mathbf{t}, \mathbf{f}) = \top$, $lub(\mathbf{t_c}, \mathbf{f_d}) = \mathbf{t_a}$, etc. Intuitively, the ground database atoms A for which $A: \mathbf{t_a}$ or $A: \mathbf{f_a}$ become true are to be inserted into, resp., deleted from D. Navigation in the lattice plus an adequate definition of APC-formula satisfaction help solve the conflicts between database atoms and constraints.

We consider only Herbrand structures [Lloyd, 1987], i.e., sets of ground annotated atoms, with the database domain as their universe. Next, formula satisfaction is defined as follows. For a structure I, $\mathbf{s} \in Lat$, and A a classical atomic formula: $I \models A\!:\!\mathbf{s}$ iff there is $\mathbf{s}' \in Lat$, such that $A\!:\!\mathbf{s}' \in I$, and $\mathbf{s} \leq \mathbf{s}'$. For other formulas, satisfaction is defined inductively, as in classical FO predicate logic.

Given an instance D and a set IC of universal ICs in clausal form, we can generate an APC-theory, $Spec$, that embeds both D and IC. This process is shown by means of an example.

Example 4.11   Consider the following functional dependencies IC:

$$Employee(x, y, z) \wedge Employee(x, u, v) \rightarrow y = u,$$
$$Employee(x, y, z) \wedge Employee(x, u, v) \rightarrow z = v,$$

and the inconsistent instance:

D	Employee	Name	Position	Salary
		Steven Lerman	ceo	4000
		Irwin Pearson	salesman	2000
		Irwin Pearson	salesman	2500
		John Miller	salesman	1600

1. For example, the first constraint is first transformed into clausal form:

$$\neg Employee(x, y, z) \vee \neg Employee(x, u, v) \vee y = u ,$$

and next, into an APC-sentence:

$$Employee(x, y, z)\!:\!\mathbf{f_c} \vee Employee(x, u, v)\!:\!\mathbf{f_c} \vee (y = u)\!:\!\mathbf{t} .$$

2. The database atoms are represented as: $Employee(Steven\ Lerman,\ ceo, 4000)\!:\!\mathbf{t_d}$, etc.

3. For every database predicate two sentences are created, imposing the uniqueness of the constraint truth value:

$$Employee(x, y, z)\!:\!\mathbf{t_c} \vee Employee(x, y, z)\!:\!\mathbf{f_c},$$
$$\neg(Employee(x, y, z)\!:\!\mathbf{t_c}) \vee \neg(Employee(x, y, z)\!:\!\mathbf{f_c}).$$

4. Closed-world-assumption:

$$Employee(x, y, z)\!:\!\mathbf{f_d} \vee (x = Steven\ Lerman\!:\!\mathbf{t_d} \wedge y = ceo\!:\!\mathbf{t_d} \wedge z = 4000\!:\!\mathbf{t_d}) \vee$$
$$(x = Irwin\ Pearson\!:\!\mathbf{t_d} \wedge y = salesman\!:\!\mathbf{t_d} \wedge z = 2000\!:\!\mathbf{t_d}) \vee$$
$$(x = Irwin\ Pearson\!:\!\mathbf{t_d} \wedge y = salesman\!:\!\mathbf{t_d} \wedge z = 2500\!:\!\mathbf{t_d}) \vee$$
$$(x = John\ Miller\!:\!\mathbf{t_d} \wedge y = salesman\!:\!\mathbf{t_d} \wedge z = 1600\!:\!\mathbf{t_d}).$$

5. Equality theory:
      True   built-in   atoms: $(Steven\ Lerman = Steven\ Lerman)\!:\!\mathbf{t}$, $(ceo = ceo)\!:\!\mathbf{t}$, $(2000 = 2000)\!:\!\mathbf{t}$, etc.

False built-in atoms: $(\textit{Steve Lerman} = \textit{Irwin Pearson}):\mathbf{f}$, $(\textit{Irwin Pearson} = \textit{Steve Lerman}):\mathbf{f}$, $(\textit{ceo} = \textit{salesman}):\mathbf{f}$, $(\textit{salesman} = \textit{ceo}):\mathbf{f}$, etc.

The axiom: $\neg(x = y:\top)$. ∎

Every model of *Spec* assigns one of the values $\mathbf{t}$, $\mathbf{f}$, $\mathbf{t_a}$, $\mathbf{f_a}$ to the atoms. In particular, it can be proved that an atom in a model of the theory is never annotated with $\top$ [Arenas et al., 2000], that is, the APC-theory is *epistemologically* consistent [Kifer and Lozinskii, 1992]. More importantly, it is possible to prove that the minimal models of *Spec* with respect to the set of annotations $\alpha = \{\mathbf{t_a}, \mathbf{f_a}\}$ correspond to the repairs of the database. More precisely, the database repairs correspond to the models of *Spec* that make true a minimal set of atoms with annotations in α. In other terms, the comparison between models is wrt to set-inclusion of the sets of atoms with annotations in α. This captures, as expected, that only a minimal set of atoms is changed (deleted or inserted).

More precisely, for an α-minimal model $\mathcal{M}$ of *Spec*,

$$D_{\mathcal{M}} = \{P(\bar{t}) \mid \mathcal{M} \models P(\bar{t}):\mathbf{t} \lor P(\bar{t}):\mathbf{t_a}\}$$

is a repair of D; and every repair can be obtained in this way. Reasoning with minimal models of *Spec* makes reasoning non-monotonic, as expected.

Example 4.12 (Example 4.11 continued) The minimal models of *Spec* are:

$\mathcal{M}_1 = \{\textit{Employee}(\textit{Steven Lerman}, \textit{ceo}, 4000):\mathbf{t}, \textit{Employee}(\textit{Irwin Pearson}, \textit{salesman}, 2000):\mathbf{t},$
$\textit{Employee}(\textit{Irwin Pearson}, \textit{salesman}, 2500):\mathbf{f_a}, \textit{Employee}(\textit{John Miller}, \textit{salesman}, 1600):\mathbf{t}\},$

$\mathcal{M}_2 = \{\textit{Employee}(\textit{Steven Lerman}, \textit{ceo}, 4000):\mathbf{t}, \textit{Employee}(\textit{Irwin Pearson}, \textit{salesman}, 2000):\mathbf{f_a},$
$\textit{Employee}(\textit{Irwin Pearson}, \textit{salesman}, 2500):\mathbf{t}, \textit{Employee}(\textit{John Miller}, \textit{salesman}, 1600):\mathbf{t}\},$

which lead to the two expected database repairs. Each of them deletes one of the original tuples involving *Steven Lerman*. ∎

Relational queries $\mathcal{Q}(\bar{x})$ waiting for consistent answers can be transformed into APC-queries $\mathcal{Q}^{an}(\bar{x})$, to be posed to the APC-theory [Barceló and Bertossi, 2002, Barceló et al., 2003]. This is done by simultaneously replacing in $\mathcal{Q}(\bar{x})$: (a) positive database literals $P(\bar{s})$ by $P(\bar{s}):\mathbf{t} \lor P(\bar{s}):\mathbf{t_a}$; (b) negative database literals $\neg P(\bar{s})$ by $P(\bar{s}):\mathbf{f} \lor P(\bar{s}):\mathbf{f_a}$; (c) built-in literals $B(\bar{s})$ by $B(\bar{s}):\mathbf{t}$.

Example 4.13 (Example 4.11 continued) If we want the consistent answers to the query

$$\mathcal{Q}(x):\ \exists y \exists z \exists w \exists t \,(\textit{Employee}(x, y, z) \land \textit{Employee}(x, w, t) \land y \neq w)\,,$$

we generate the APC-query:

$$\mathcal{Q}^{an}(\bar{x}):\ \exists y \exists z \exists w \exists t \,((\textit{Employee}(x, y, z):\mathbf{t} \lor \textit{Employee}(x, y, z):\mathbf{t_a}) \land$$
$$(\textit{Employee}(x, w, t):\mathbf{t} \lor \textit{Employee}(x, w, t):\mathbf{t_a}) \land (y \neq w):\mathbf{t})).$$

This query has to be posed to the APC-theory *Spec*, and be answered according to the truth in all the α-minimal models of *Spec*. ∎

In more general terms, it holds [Barceló and Bertossi, 2002, Barceló et al., 2003]:

$$D \models_{IC} \mathcal{Q}(\bar{t}) \text{ iff } Spec \models_\alpha \mathcal{Q}^{an}(\bar{t}) ,$$

where, on the right-hand side, we have truth wrt α-minimal models of *Spec*. This non-monotonic entailment relation reflects the non-monotonicity of consistent query answering.

4.3   SECOND-ORDER REPRESENTATIONS

In the first two sections, we have seen logical specifications of repairs in non-classical logical formalisms. With the general goal of better understanding the logics of CQA, a natural question is whether repairs can be represented in classical logic. Actually, for complexity-theoretic reasons (cf. Chapter 5), it should be possible to specify the class of repairs in second-order (SO) classical predicate logic, where variables and quantifiers for predicates (to range over relations on the domain) are also allowed.

A concrete SO specification can be obtained from a repair program of the kind presented in Section 4.1. This is based on the fact that the stable model semantics of disjunctive logic programs, in general, can be recovered via a classical SO theory. The latter is in essence a *circumscriptive characterization* of the stable models of such a logic program, and can be effectively produced from the program [Ferraris et al., 2011]. Circumscription was introduced in knowledge representation by McCarthy [1980] (cf. also [Lifschitz, 1994]) as way of imposing the minimization of the predicate extensions; and by doing so, of capturing common sense assumptions and reasoning.

Bertossi [2009] applies this transformation to repair programs and investigates the issue in the context of CQA. We will illustrate the approach by means of an example (details can be found in [Bertossi, 2009]).

Example 4.14   Consider the following relational schema with an FD: $P(X, Y) : X \rightarrow Y$, and the inconsistent instance $D = \{P(a, b), P(a, c), P(d, e)\}$.

In this case, we can use this simple repair program:

$$\begin{aligned}
P\_(x, y, \mathbf{f_a}) \vee P\_(x, z, \mathbf{f_a}) \quad &\leftarrow \quad P(x, y), \ P(x, z), \ y \neq z. \qquad (4.5) \\
P\_(x, y, \mathbf{t}^{\star\star}) \quad &\leftarrow \quad P(x, y), \ not \ P\_(x, y, \mathbf{f_a}).
\end{aligned}$$
$$P(a, b). \ P(a, c). \ P(d, e).$$

This program can be seen as a FO specification, namely the FO conjunction Ψ_ρ of the following sentences (assuming the formulas are universally closed):

$$\begin{aligned}
P(x, y) \wedge P(x, z) \wedge y \neq z \quad &\rightarrow \quad P_f(x, y) \vee P_f(x, z). \\
P(x, y) \wedge \neg P_f(x, y) \quad &\rightarrow \quad P_{\star\star}(x, y).
\end{aligned}$$
$$P(a, b) \wedge P(a, c) \wedge P(d, e). \qquad\qquad\qquad\qquad \blacksquare$$

It is possible to assign a stable model semantics to any FO sentence Ψ [Ferraris et al., 2011]. More precisely, a SO sentence Ψ' can be built, with the same signature as Ψ. The stable models of Ψ are, by definition, the Herbrand models of Ψ', which is called *the stable sentence* of Ψ. Actually, for disjunctive logic programs seen as FO specifications (as in the example above), this stable semantics coincides with their original stable model semantics.

Example 4.15   (Example 4.14 continued) In this case, Ψ'_ρ becomes

$$\forall xy(P(x, y) \equiv (x = a \land y = b) \lor (x = a \land y = c) \lor (x = d \land y = e)) \ \land \tag{4.6}$$
$$\forall xy((P(x, y) \land \neg P_f(x, y)) \equiv P_{\star\star}(x, y)) \ \land \tag{4.7}$$
$$\forall xyz(P(x, y) \land P(x, z) \land y \neq z \to (P_f(x, y) \lor P_f(x, z)) \ \land$$
$$\neg \exists U((U < P_f) \land \forall xyz(P(x, y) \land P(x, z) \land y \neq z \to (U(x, y) \lor U(x, z)))). \tag{4.8}$$

This sentence includes, in (4.6), Reiter's logical reconstruction of the instance [Reiter, 1984]; and Clark's predicate completion of predicate P [Lloyd, 1987]. Predicate P_f is minimized via the last conjunct (4.8) of Ψ'_ρ. It is a circumscription of the predicate P_f that contains the deleted tuples. Here, $U < P_f$ is an abbreviation for the formula $\forall xy(U(x, y) \to P_f(x, y)) \land \exists xy(P_f(x, y) \land \neg U(x, y))$. Second-order logic, represented by the quantifier $\exists U$, captures this minimization process. ∎

More generally, the stable sentence for a repair program (as a FO sentence Ψ_ρ) is always a circumscription in parallel of all the predicates in the program. However, due to the structure of a repair program (including the query program), the circumscription becomes a *prioritized circumscription* [Lifschitz, 1994]. In the example, the predicates are minimized in this order: 1. Database predicates. 2. Predicates with $\mathbf{f_a}$ annotation. 3. Predicates with $\mathbf{t^{\star\star}}$ annotation. 4. The *Ans* predicate.

Most complex is the minimization of predicates defined by disjunctive rules, i.e., those associated to the ICs. To all the others, it is possible to apply predicate completion, as with sentence (4.7) in the example.

Example 4.16   (Example 4.15 continued) Now we want to consistently answer query $\mathcal{Q}(x, y): P(x, y)$. This amounts to obtaining the pairs $\langle a, b \rangle$, such that:

$$\Psi'_\rho \ \land \ \forall x \forall y(Ans(x, y) \equiv P_{\star\star}(x, y)) \ \models \ Ans(a, b), \tag{4.9}$$

which is classical logical entailment in SO predicate logic.

A natural question is whether it is possible to rely on classical FO logic, at least in some cases. In this direction we can try to use (4.9), obtaining entailment in FO logic via elimination of SO quantifiers from Ψ'_ρ. There are some techniques available for this task. Bertossi [2009] applies those techniques that are proposed by Doherty et al. [1997]. This requires having sentence (4.8) in a particular syntactic form that requires the use of a Skolem function [Lloyd, 1987], the symbolic function g in (4.10), below.

The negation of (4.8) is logically equivalent to:

$$\exists s \exists t \exists g \exists U \forall x \forall r\, (\forall x_1 y_1 z_1(\neg \kappa(x_1, y_1, z_1) \vee g(x_1, y_1, z_1) = \vee(y_1, z_1)) \wedge \qquad (4.10)$$
$$\forall yz(\neg \kappa(x, y, z) \vee r \neq g(x, y, z) \vee U(x, r))) \wedge$$
$$\forall uv(\neg U(u, v) \vee P_f(u, v)) \wedge (P_f(s, t) \wedge \neg U(s, t))).$$

Here, $\kappa(x, y, z)$ stands for $P(x, y) \wedge P(x, z) \wedge y \neq z$, a violation of the FD; and $t = \vee(t_1, t_2)$ stands for $t = t_1 \vee t = t_2$.

Now we are in position to apply Ackermann's lemma [Doherty et al., 1997], because the formula is of the form (below we will make reference to the underlined part of it)

$$\underline{\exists s \exists t \exists g \exists U \forall x \forall r((A(x, r) \vee U(x, r)) \wedge B\frac{U}{\neg U}}),\qquad (4.11)$$

with

$$A(x, r): \quad \forall yz(\forall yz(\neg \kappa(x, y, z) \vee r \neq g(x, y, z)),$$
$$B(U): \quad \forall x_1 y_1 z_1(\neg \kappa(x_1, y_1, z_1) \vee g(x_1, y_1, z_1) = \vee(y_1, z_1)) \wedge$$
$$\forall uv(U(u, v) \vee P_f(u, v)) \wedge (P_f(s, t) \wedge U(s, t)));$$

$B\frac{U}{\neg U}$ being formula B with predicate U replaced by $\neg U$, and B positive in U.

Under these conditions, the underlined subformula in (4.11) can be equivalently replaced by $B\frac{U}{A(x,r)}$, obtaining:

$$\exists s \exists t \exists g(\forall x_1 y_1 z_1(\neg \kappa(x_1, y_1, z_1) \vee g(x_1, y_1, z_1) = \vee(y_1, z_1)) \wedge$$
$$\forall uv(\forall yz(\neg \kappa(u, y, z) \vee v \neq g(u, y, z) \vee P_f(u, v)) \wedge$$
$$(P_f(s, t) \wedge \forall y_1 z_1(\neg \kappa(s, y_1, z_1) \vee t \neq g(s, y_1, z_1))).$$

Unskolemizing, i.e., eliminating the function symbol g by introducing FO universal quantifiers followed by existential quantifiers, we obtain:

$$\exists s \exists t \forall x y z \exists w((\neg \kappa(x, y, z) \vee w = \vee(y, z)) \wedge$$
$$(\neg \kappa(x, y, z) \vee P_f(u, w)) \wedge (P_f(s, t) \wedge (x \neq s \vee \neg \kappa(x, y, z) \vee t \neq w))).$$

The negation of this formula is equivalent, via other conjuncts in (4.6)–(4.8), to

$$\forall st(P_f(s, t) \rightarrow \exists xyz \forall w(\kappa(x, y, z) \wedge (P_f(x, w) \rightarrow (x = s \wedge t = w)))),$$

which can be replaced for (4.8), obtaining an equivalent FO specification of predicate P_f. This is a FO theory Ψ_ρ'' we can do CQA with. In this case, to find the $\langle a, b \rangle$s, such that

$$\Psi_\rho'' \wedge \forall xy(Ans(x, y) \equiv P_{\star\star}(x, y)) \models Ans(a, b).\qquad (4.12)$$

This is classical FO entailment. Actually, in this case, through a simple logically equivalent transformation, it is possible to obtain from (4.12):

$$D \models (P(x, y) \wedge \neg \exists z(P(x, z) \wedge z \neq y)[a, b],$$

reobtaining the original FO rewriting we had in (3.1). ■

The methodology we have just sketched, provably works for functional dependencies (and key constraints). However, this does not imply that CQA can be done in polynomial time in these cases, because we have a theory on the left-hand side of (4.12), not a database instance.

As a more general methodology, possibly applicable to other classes of ICs, it has to be further investigated. It essence is the following: The query is posed on top of a FO specification of repairs, and the database instance (or its completion) lies at the bottom. Thus, CQA becomes something like query answering in databases with complex, expressive and implicitly defined FO views.

CHAPTER 5

Decision Problems in CQA: Complexity and Algorithms

In this chapter we start by presenting some time complexity results for tuple-oriented and set-inclusion based repairs for FO queries and ICs (cf. Section 5.1). We also briefly discuss the role of aggregation (cf. Section 5.6). We take advantage of the general complexity analysis to both introduce cardinality-based and attribute-based repairs (cf. Sections 5.7 and 5.8, respectively), and investigate the corresponding complexity of CQA .

5.1 THE DECISION PROBLEMS

In previous chapters we have pointed to the fact that first-order query rewriting gives us a polynomial time algorithm for computing consistent answers. In this section we will summarize some of the complexity results that have been obtained for CQA. Until further notice, we will concentrate on tuple- and set-inclusion-based repairs (cf. Section 2.5.1).

As usual in data management, we concentrate mostly on *data complexity* [Abiteboul et al., 1995, Vardi, 1982]. That is, we consider the schema, the query and the set of ICs as fixed parameters, making only the database instance D vary as an instance for the computational problem, usually a decision problem, as in (5.2) below. Thus, the computational complexity, usually time complexity, depends upon and is measured in terms of the size of D. When we consider in the complexity analysis also other variables for the computational problem, e.g., the query and/or the ICs, we talk about *combined complexity* (cf. 5.5) [Vardi, 1982].

More precisely, we focus on the *decision problem of CQA*, namely about deciding if a tuple is a consistent answer to a query $\mathcal{Q}(\bar{x})$:

$$CQA(\mathcal{Q}, IC) := \{(D, \bar{t}) \mid D \models_{IC} \mathcal{Q}[\bar{t}]\}. \tag{5.1}$$

Here, both the set of ICs and the query are fixed parameters of the problem, and the variable input (or instance) of the decision problem is the database instance D. That is, we want to estimate the time it takes to decide about a tuple being a consistent answer as a function of the size of D.

Actually, to study the complexity of CQA, it is good enough to concentrate on boolean queries since, as it is easy to see, moving to queries with free variables will not cause *CQA* to shift from polynomial to exponential complexity, because the free variables can only be instantiated in polynomially many ways. In consequence, for a boolean query $\mathcal{Q}$ the decision problem (5.1) becomes

$$CQA(\mathcal{Q}, IC) := \{D \mid D \models_{IC} \mathcal{Q}\}. \tag{5.2}$$

The computational problem becomes the one of deciding if instance D makes the sentence Q consistently true wrt IC; and time complexity is measured only terms of the size of D.

In Section 5.5, we consider *combined complexity* of CQA, i.e., as a function of combinations of several inputs, e.g., both the instance and the query (for a fixed set of ICs).

The repair logic programs discussed in Chapter 4 provide declarative and executable specifications of database repairs. We made the observation there that this kind of specification of repairs, extended with query programs, provide a form of query rewriting. It transforms the original first-order query Q into a query $\Pi(D, IC) \cup \Pi(Q)$, that is expressed in a more complex language than the one of Q. The database instance D over which Q is posed, expecting consistent answers, is essentially the same as the one used by the program $\Pi(D, IC) \cup \Pi(Q)$, which is run on top of D.

These observations give us immediately an upper bound on the data complexity of CQA. More precisely, whenever the repair program $\Pi(D, IC)$ correctly specifies $Rep(D, IC)$, it holds

$$(D, \bar{t}) \in CQA(Q, IC) \text{ iff } \Pi(D, IC) \cup \Pi(Q) \models_{sk} Ans(\bar{t}) .$$

On the right-hand side we have a decision problem of skeptical query evaluation over a disjunctive program with stable model semantics. The program has a fixed set of rules (coming from IC and Q) and a variable set of facts D. Thus, we are dealing with data complexity. This problem is known to be Π_2^P-complete [Dantsin et al., 2001].

A problem that is natural to consider, and that happens to be closely related to CQA, is repair checking. It sheds light on the complexity of CQA. More precisely, the *repair checking problem* is the following decision problem:

$$RCH(IC) := \{(D, D') \mid D' \text{ is a repair of } D \text{ wrt } IC\}. \tag{5.3}$$

Again, here we have the problem parameterized by the set of ICs. The pairs formed by the original instance and a candidate to be repair become the inputs to the problem. So, we are also considering data complexity.

It is easy to see that there is a connection between the repair checking and the consistent query answering problems. Notice that, in order to decide if a tuple $\bar{t}$ *is not* a consistent answer to a query, we can *guess a repair* D' and verify, in polynomial time, that D' does not make the query true with tuple $\bar{t}$. Thus, the complexity of CQA depends on the complexity of repair checking.

5.2   SOME UPPER BOUNDS

As with CQA, we can obtain a complexity upper-bound for repair checking from the specification of repairs as the stable models of a disjunctive logic program: The complexity of checking if a subset of the Herbrand base [Lloyd, 1987] is a stable model of the disjunctive program is *coNP*-complete in data [Dantsin et al., 2001]. We obtain the *coNP* upper-bound for *RCH*. Since this is the test we invoked above for the complement of *CQA*, we (re)obtain that *CQA* belongs to the class Π_2^P, that is one level above *coNP* in the *polynomial hierarchy* [Johnson, 1990, Papadimitriou, 1994] (c.f. Figure 5.1).

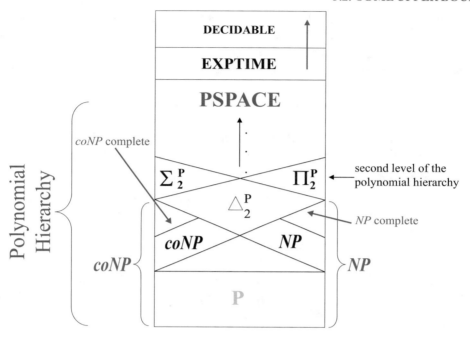

Figure 5.1: The polynomial hierarchy (and above).

Summarizing, we have the complexity upper-bounds of *coNP* and Π_2^P for the problems *RCH* and *CQA*, respectively. Next, the natural question is whether these problems are *complete* for these classes. Actually, as we will see below, they are. This shows that the logic programming-based approach to CQA (and repair checking) is not an overkill, at least for the hard cases of *RCH* and *CQA*.

Before addressing completeness for those decision problems and their classes, we can try to take some more advantage from the repair programs. It happens that there are classes of disjunctive programs for which repair checking and skeptical query evaluation have both lower complexity than for the general case, namely *PTIME* and *coNP*, respectively.[1] This is the case of the *head-cycle free programs* (HCF).

A disjunctive program Π is associated to a directed graph $\mathcal{G}(\Pi)$ which is built by first considering the ground or instantiated version Π^g of Π, as follows.

1. Each ground literal is a node.

2. There is an edge from A to A' iff there is a rule in Π^g where A appears positive in the body and A' in its head.

---

[1]Under the usual complexity theoretic assumption that the polynomial hierarchy does not collapse [Johnson, 1990].

By definition, Π is HCF iff $\mathcal{G}(\Pi)$ has no cycles with two literals belonging to the head of the same rule. A HCF program Π can be transformed into a (non-disjunctive) normal program with the same stable models [Dantsin et al., 2001], and, as a consequence, query answering under skeptical semantics becomes *coNP* (actually, complete for this class); and stable model checking belongs to *PTIME*.

Barceló et al. [2003] identify some common classes of ICs for which the repair programs become HCF. This is the case for denial constraints, and in particular, for functional dependencies (FDs) and key constraints. Thus, for denial constraints *RCH* is in *PTIME*, and *CQA* in *coNP*. For example, the disjunctive rule in (4.5) for an FD can be transformed into a pair of non-disjunctive rules, by moving in turn each of the disjuncts in negated form to the body:

$$P\_(x, y, \mathbf{f_a}) \quad \leftarrow \quad P(x, y), \; P(x, z), \; y \neq z, \; not \; P\_(x, z, \mathbf{f_a}).$$
$$P\_(x, z, \mathbf{f_a}) \quad \leftarrow \quad P(x, y), \; P(x, z), \; y \neq z, \; not \; P\_(x, y, \mathbf{f_a}).$$

In this case, any one of the two rules is sufficient.

We have obtained upper bounds for the two main decision problems related to CQA. Next, it is natural to ask about completeness for these complexity classes or about lower bounds for the complexity of these problems. The first results of this kind are due to Arenas et al. [2003b], for FDs and aggregate queries (cf. Section 5.6), and to Chomicki and Marcinkowski [2005] for first-order queries.

For FDs, repair checking can be done in polynomial time in the size of the given instance D and the repair candidate D' [Chomicki and Marcinkowski, 2005]. Intuitively, for each tuple in $(D \setminus D')$ it can be checked if it can be consistently added to D'. If none of those tuples can be added, then D' is a minimal repair of D (assuming that D' does not violate any of the FDs, which can be efficiently checked first). In essence, this amounts to checking that D' satisfies the FDs, and that it minimally differs from D, i.e., that it is a maximal consistent subset of D wrt set inclusion. Minimality tests of this kind can be expensive [Eiter and Gottlob, 1992]. Accordingly, this becomes the most expensive part of repair checking.

The polynomial time of repair checking for FDs, and the algorithmic idea behind, can be extended to denial constraints in general [Chomicki and Marcinkowski, 2005, Theo. 3.1]. A systematic and complete analysis of repair checking, and for different repair semantics, is given by Afrati and Kolaitis [2009].

5.3   SOME LOWER BOUNDS

As indicated above, for a fixed set of FDs and a FO query $\mathcal{Q}$, an algorithm to check if a tuple $\bar{t}$ is *not* a consistent answer to $\mathcal{Q}$ in D consists in first guessing a repair D', which, as we just saw, can be verified in polynomial time, and then checking that $D' \not\models \mathcal{Q}[\bar{t}]$. This tells us that the complementary problem, i.e., CQA, can be solved *coNP* time. Actually, CQA turns out to be *hard* for this class [Chomicki and Marcinkowski, 2005]. More precisely, there are sets of FDs, *FD*, and queries $\mathcal{Q}$ for which $CQA(\mathcal{Q}, FD)$ becomes *coNP*-complete. Actually, a one predicate schema with a single key constraint and a boolean conjunctive query (with projection) suffice for this result [Chomicki and Marcinkowski, 2005, Theo. 3.3].

We will illustrate the idea of the proof since it shows well the form of reasoning involved in results of this kind (details can be found in [Chomicki and Marcinkowski, 2005]).

We fix a schema $\mathcal{S} = \{R(A, B, C)\}$, with a single predicate, and also the key constraint $KC : A \to BC$. The query is also fixed, namely

$$\mathcal{Q} : \exists x \exists y \exists z (R(x, y, c) \land R(z, y, d)), \tag{5.4}$$

where c, d are constants in the database domain. With all these elements the problem

$$CQA^c := \{D \mid D \text{ is instance for } \mathcal{S} \text{ and } D \not\models_{\{KC\}} \mathcal{Q}\},$$

i.e., the complement of CQA, becomes *NP*-hard. This claim can be proved by reducing the *NP*-complete problem *MON-SAT* in polynomial time to CQA^c. That is, each input instance for *MON-SAT*, i.e., a conjunction of propositional clauses where all the literals in a clause are either simultaneously positive or simultaneously negative, can be mapped to an input instance for CQA^c, preserving membership.

For example, the propositional formula φ : $(p \lor q \lor r) \land (\neg p \lor \neg q)$ is mapped to the database instance $D = \{R(1, p, c), R(1, q, c), R(1, r, c), R(2, p, d), R(2, q, d)\}$. The first attribute value indicates the clause number, and the second, a propositional variable appearing in it. With c and d we tell apart the positive and negative clauses. D is clearly inconsistent. Furthermore, φ is satisfiable iff $D \not\models_{\{KC\}} \mathcal{Q}$ iff D has a repair D' such that $D \not\models \mathcal{Q}$. In this case, φ is satisfiable, and a repair D' with this property is $D' = \{R(1, p, c), R(2, q, d)\}$.

Notice that since we are interested in data complexity, the input instance for *MON-SAT* has to be encoded through the database instance while keeping the schema, IC and query all fixed.

It is also worth noticing that, as expected, the query in (5.4) does not fall in the syntactic tractable class $\mathcal{C}_{Tree}$ introduced in Section 3.4. The same predicate appears twice in the query.

Obviously, this *coNP*-completeness result implies *coNP*-completeness of CQA for the class of denial constraints and conjunctive queries. Other combinations of key constraints (or denial constraints) and queries can be used to obtain this same result [Chomicki and Marcinkowski, 2005]. These are worst-case complexity results, and, as we have seen in Chapter 3, there are cases of queries and denial constraints for which CQA can be done in polynomial time.

Higher complexity classes can be reached by considering other kinds of ICs. Chomicki and Marcinkowski [2005] consider the combination of FDs and inclusion dependencies, and the latter are repaired by tuple deletions (cf. Section 2.5.2). These inclusion dependencies may contain existential quantifiers in the consequent, but value inventions are not used to restore consistency. In this case, repair checking becomes *coNP*-complete, and the non-acyclicity of the set of inclusion dependencies is used to establish this result [Chomicki and Marcinkowski, 2005, Theo. 4.6]. As we argued at the beginning of this section, this makes CQA (for this kind of ICs and repair semantics) belong to the class Π_2^P. Actually, CQA becomes Π_2^P-complete [Chomicki and Marcinkowski, 2005, Theo. 4.7].

The complexity analysis of CQA under tuple-based and set-oriented repairs is extended by Staworko and Chomicki [2010] to the whole class of universal constraints. This class of ICs goes beyond denial constraints, including, among other classes of ICs, full-tuple generation dependencies, which include *full inclusion dependencies*, i.e., sentences of the form $\forall \bar{x}(R(\bar{x}) \to S(\bar{x}'))$, with $\bar{x}' \subseteq \bar{x}$ (non-full inclusion dependencies introduce existential quantifiers), and also *join dependencies*, in particular, *multi-valued dependencies* [Abiteboul et al., 1995]. In contrast to [Chomicki and Marcinkowski, 2005], Staworko and Chomicki [2010] consider the solution of violations of inclusion dependencies via tuple insertions or deletions (the same applies to any other universal constraint that allows for both possibilities). That is, the repair semantics is exactly as in [Arenas et al., 1999]. The queries considered are boolean conjunctions of atoms.

Staworko and Chomicki [2010] extend the conflict-hypergraph representation of repairs introduced in [Chomicki and Marcinkowski, 2005] to obtain polynomial time algorithms for the generation of all repairs and repair checking for full tuple generation dependencies and denial constraints, and also for CQA for boolean queries without quantifiers and join dependencies, *acyclic* full tuple generating dependencies, and denial constraints. They also establish that CQA becomes *coNP*-complete for boolean atomic queries and arbitrary full-tuple generating dependencies and denial constraints. However, for the same kind of queries, but arbitrary universal constraints, CQA becomes Π_2^P-complete. This last result [Staworko and Chomicki, 2010, Theo. 6] includes the Π_2^P-hardness for a fixed set of universal constraints, namely two FDs and a *disjunctive constraint*, i.e., of the form $\forall \bar{x}(D(\bar{x}) \to R_1(\bar{x}_1) \vee R_2(\bar{x}_2) \vee R_3(\bar{x}_3) \vee R_4(\bar{x}_4))$, with $\bar{x}_i \subseteq \bar{x}$.

Calì et al. [2003] investigate the combination of key dependencies and inclusion dependencies, i.e., of the form $R[A_1, \cdots, A_n] \subseteq S[B_1, \ldots, B_n]$. Since $A_1, \cdots, A_n$ and $B_1, \ldots, B_n$ are not necessarily all the attributes of R, resp. S, this class includes referential constraints. Repairs are based on insertion/deletion of tuples and are also set-oriented. Under the so-called *sound semantics*, violations of inclusion dependencies are solved via tuple insertions (cf. Section 2.5.3). This reflects the view of an instance as an *open* or *incomplete* set of tuples. Under these assumptions, CQA becomes undecidable [Calì et al., 2003, Theo. 3.4]. Here, both the schema, the ICs, the query and the instance are input to the decision problem. Crucial elements for this result are the interaction of KDs and existentially quantified inclusion dependencies, the possibly infinite underlying domain used for value invention, and cycles in the set of inclusion dependencies (cf. Section 5.5 for a more precise statement of this result).

Next, Calì et al. [2003] study CQA for a large class of KDs and inclusion dependencies that does not exhibit the kind of interaction that leads to undecidability. That is the class of KDs plus *non-key conflicting* inclusion dependencies, i.e., such that none of them propagates a proper subset of the key of the relation in its right-hand side (i.e., $B_1, \ldots, B_n$ is not a proper subset of the key for S above). For this class of constraints, CQA becomes decidable, and its complexity makes it: (a) *PSPACE*-complete in combined complexity (cf. Section 5.5 for more on combined complexity), and (b) an element of *PTIME* in data complexity [Calì et al., 2003, Theo. 3.9].

We conclude this section pointing to the fact that, when referential constraints are repaired with non-propagating SQL nulls (cf. Section 2.5.4), for arbitrary universal ICs and even cyclic sets of inclusion dependencies, the decidability of CQA is restored. Actually, CQA becomes Π_2^P-complete [Bravo and Bertossi, 2006].

5.4 FO REWRITING VS. PTIME AND ABOVE

As discussed in Chapter 3, in those cases where there are FO consistent query rewritings, CQA can be done in *PTIME*. On the other side, the results described in the previous section show that FO query rewriting has limited applicability. A natural question about this methodology is whether it can be applied to all cases where CQA can be done *PTIME*.

Wijsen [2009b] shows an example of a boolean conjunctive query, namely $Q : \exists x \exists y (R(\underline{x}, y) \wedge R(\underline{y}, c))$ (with the intended key-constraints underlined), that can be consistently answered in *PTIME*, but provably has no FO consistent rewriting.

This non-expressibility or non-definability result uses a proof technique based on Ehrenfeucht-Fraïssé (EF) games [Ebbinghaus et al., 1994]. It is particularly suitable when the models involved, like relational databases, are finite [Abiteboul et al., 1995].

The general idea is to use EF games to establish that two concrete database instances share the same FO-definable properties within a class that would include the FO consistent rewriting of the query if it existed. Next, one verifies that the two instances have different consistent answers. This proves that such a FO rewriting cannot exist.

EF games (and their generalizations) are among the fundamental tools for establishing non-definability results in formal logics. They belong to the essential toolkit of the database theorists [Libkin, 2009], and more generally, of the finite-model theorists [Ebbinghaus and Flum, 2005, Libkin, 2004, Makowsky, 2008].

This issue of *PTIME* vs. FO rewriting for CQA was first raised by Fuxman and Miller [2003], where it is claimed that the query $Q : \exists x \exists y \exists z (R(\underline{x}, z) \wedge R(\underline{y}, z) \wedge x \neq y)$ can be consistently answered in *PTIME*, but has no FO consistent rewriting.

Most of the results we have mentioned so far in this section can be seen from a higher-level perspective, as contributions to two more general problems that have started to be addressed [Pema et al., 2011, Wijsen, 2010b], namely:

(A) Find an algorithm that takes as input a boolean FO query Q (with a given set of key constraints *KC* which are indicated together with the query), and decides whether $CQA(Q)$ is FO definable.

(B) Find an algorithm that takes as input a boolean FO query Q, and decides whether $CQA(Q)$ is in *PTIME* or *coNP*-complete (i.e., tractable or intractable). Notice that neither may be the case if *PTIME* $\neq$ *coNP*.

Most research on the above problems (A) and (B) has focused on conjunctive queries. Additional restrictions are often imposed: (a) Q must be acyclic in the sense of Beeri et al. [1983]; and/or (b) Q has no self-join, meaning that every relation name occurs at most once in Q.

The problem (A) has been solved under these restrictions, that is, when $\mathcal{Q}$ ranges over the class of acyclic conjunctive queries without self-joins [Wijsen, 2010b]. Moreover, for this class of queries, the decision boundaries in (A) and (B) do not coincide: For the conjunctive query $\mathcal{Q} : \exists x \exists y (R(\underline{x}, y) \wedge S(\underline{y}, x))$, it is the case that $CQA(\mathcal{Q})$ is in *PTIME*, but not first-order definable [Wijsen, 2010a]. This is the first example of a conjunctive query without self-joins with this property. More (conjunctive, two-atom, and self-join free) queries with this property have later been identified by Pema et al. [2011]. These results generalize and improve work started by Fuxman and Miller [2005, 2007]. The class of acyclic conjunctive queries without self-joins, notwithstanding its restrictions, remains a large class of practical interest.

Relatively little is known about $CQA(\mathcal{Q})$ for conjunctive queries $\mathcal{Q}$ that are cyclic and/or contain self-joins. As mentioned in Section 3.4, first-order definability of $CQA(\mathcal{Q})$ is guaranteed for all conjunctive queries $\mathcal{Q}$ belonging to the semantic class of *key-rooted* conjunctive queries. Key-rooted queries can be cyclic and contain self-joins. However, no algorithm is known to test whether a conjunctive query is key-rooted.

Concerning problem (B), it is an open conjecture that for every conjunctive query $\mathcal{Q}$ without self-join, it is the case that $CQA(\mathcal{Q})$ is in *PTIME* or *coNP*-complete. For a class of conjunctive queries with two atoms, a dichotomy result for CQA, i.e., about being in *PTIME* or being *coNP*-complete, has been obtained [Pema et al., 2011].

5.5 COMBINED DECIDABILITY AND COMPLEXITY

As above, we concentrate on the complexity of deciding if a boolean query $\mathcal{Q}$ is true in all repairs of an instance D wrt a set of integrity constraints IC. Most of the research so far has concentrated on data complexity, i.e., on the complexity in terms of the size, $|D|$, of D, with fixed parameters $\mathcal{Q}$ and IC. Since it is possible to consider several combinations of parameters, we will use a more precise notation for this kind of problems. For example, the one just mentioned, that leaves the query and the ICs fixed, is the decision problem

$$d\text{-}CQA(\mathcal{Q}, IC) := \{ D \mid D \models_{IC} \mathcal{Q} \} \, .$$

This problem is decidable for all classes of queries and ICs that are found or used in database practice, and the time complexity varies from P to Π_2^P-complete.

With respect to the (un)decidability for other combinations of parameters, not much was known until recently. Calì et al. [2003] establish that the problem

$$\{d, q, ic\}\text{-}CQA := \{ (D, \mathcal{Q}, IC) \mid D \models_{IC} \mathcal{Q} \}$$

is undecidable. The proof of this result relies on the following elements:

(a) A reduction from the problem of deciding entailment from sets of FDs, $\mathcal{F}$, and inclusion dependencies, $\mathcal{I}$, i.e., $\mathcal{F} \cup \mathcal{I} \models \delta$. This problem is undecidable [Abiteboul et al., 1995].

(b) The reduction requires generating $\mathcal{F}, \mathcal{I}, \delta$, in this case, a combination of key constraints, referential ICs, a query, and a database instance.

(c) The proof uses key constraints interacting with cyclic referential ICs.

(d) Referential ICs are repaired by tuple insertions, and existential quantifiers are satisfied by picking up values from the underlying domain U.

This undecidability result leaves room for the investigation of other cases of combined (un)decidability and complexity, that is cases of X-CQA, for $X \subseteq \{d, q, ic\}$. This research was undertaken in [Arenas and Bertossi, 2010]. In the rest of this section we briefly describe some of the results obtained.

There exist a database instance D and a query $\mathcal{Q}$ such that $\{ic\}$-$CQA(D, \mathcal{Q})$ is undecidable. The proof of this claim uses the following elements:

(a) A schema $\mathcal{S}$ with a binary predicate E and a unary predicate P.

(b) The instance is $D = \{P(a)\}$, with empty extension for E.

(c) The query is $\mathcal{Q}$: $\neg P(a)$.

(d) The decision problem $SAT := \{\psi \in L(\{E\}) \mid \psi$ is satisfiable$\}$ is undecidable over finite graphs, and can be reduced to the complement of ic-$CQA(D, \mathcal{Q})$.

(e) The reduction maps a FO sentence $\psi \in L(\{E\})$ to $IC := \{\psi \leftrightarrow \exists x\, P(x)\}$.

(f) It holds that $\psi \in SAT$ iff $D \not\models_{IC} \mathcal{Q}$.

It is also the case that there exists a database instance D and IC such that q-$CQA(D, IC)$ is undecidable. The proof is based on:

(a) A schema $\mathcal{S}$ with unary P, binary E, ternary F, and built-in predicate $\leq$ that is interpreted in such a way that $(U, \leq)$ is isomorphic to $(\mathbb{N}, \leq)$.

(b) The set of ICs is $IC = \{\exists x\, P(x), \forall u \forall v(E(u, v) \leftrightarrow \exists y\, F(u, v, y)), \forall x \forall y(P(x) \wedge y \leq x \rightarrow \exists u \exists v\, F(u, v, y))\}$.

(c) $D = \emptyset$.

(d) The decision problem $SAT := \{\psi \in L(\{E\}) \mid \psi$ is satisfiable$\}$, undecidable over finite graphs, can be reduced to the complement of q-$CQA(D, IC)$.

(e) It holds, $\psi \in SAT$ iff $\neg\psi \notin q$-$CQA(D, IC)$, i.e., $\psi \in SAT$ iff $D \not\models_{IC} \neg\psi$.

Now, for the last of the "singleton" cases for X in X-CQA, there exist a query Q and IC, such that d-$CQA(Q, IC)$ is undecidable. This is proved by reduction from the halting problem for deterministic Turing machines with empty string. Here, the elements of the machine, M, are captured by relational predicates, IC codifies the dynamics of the machine, as based on a generic transition function. The database instance, $D(M)$, contains the specific transition function. Repairing the instance wrt the dynamics of the machine corresponds to making the machine compute. The query asks if there is a halting state, namely Q: $\neg \exists t\ State(t, q_f)$. Undecidability is obtained, because M halts iff $D(M) \not\models_{IC} Q$.

Notice that for $Y \subseteq X$: If X-CQA is decidable, then Y-CQA also decidable. Or, contrapositively, if Y-CQA is undecidable, then X-CQA is also undecidable. As a consequence, we obtain the *general undecidability of CQA*: For every nonempty subset X of $\{d, q, ic\}$, there are cases where X-CQA is undecidable. The cases depend upon parameters of the problem, i.e., on $\{d, q, ic\} \setminus X$. A discussion of these results can be found in [Arenas and Bertossi, 2010].

Some cases of combined complexity for decidable cases are also investigated by Arenas and Bertossi [2010]. Mainly, for the relevant class of *safe universal ICs* (SU ICs), those that are logically equivalent to a sentence of the form

$$\bar{\forall}(\bigvee_{i=1}^{m} P_i(\bar{x}_i) \vee \bigvee_{j=1}^{n} \neg Q_j(\bar{y}_j) \vee \psi), \tag{5.5}$$

where each variable in an $\bar{x}_i$ or ψ appears in some of the $\bar{y}_j$. Safety is important. For example, the ICs used in the proof of the undecidability of $\{d\}$-CQA are universal, but not safe.

It holds that, for SU ICs, $\{ic, q, d\}$-CQA is decidable. The proof uses ICs of the form (5.5), and the decision procedure uses the possibly exponentially many repairs of the original database. However, the transformation from SU ICs to format (5.5) may add an additional exponent. Actually, it holds:

(A) for every boolean query Q, $\{ic, d\}$-$CQA(Q) := \{(D, \varphi) \mid \varphi$ is SU IC and $D \models_{\{\varphi\}} Q\}$ is in *co-2-NEXP*;

(B) there are boolean queries for which the same problem is *co-NEXP*-hard.

The participating complexity/decidability classes are shown in Figure 5.2, which complements Figure 5.1.

Claim (A) is obtained by proving that the complement of $\{ic, d\}$-$CQA(Q)$ belongs to *2-NEXP*. For this, one has to consider the two exponents mentioned above plus the guess of a non-satisfying repair.

Claim (B) is obtained by reduction from *SAT* for the Bernays-Schönfinkel's class (BSC) of FO sentences to the complement of $\{ic, d\}$-$CQA(Q)$. BSC contains sentences χ of the form $\exists x_1 \cdots \exists x_n \forall \bar{y}\ \psi(x_1, \ldots, x_n, \bar{y}) \in L(S)$, with ψ quantifier-free. A formula χ of this kind, if satisfiable, can be satisfied in a finite universe, with n elements. *BSC-SAT* is decidable and *NEXP*-complete [Börger et al., 2001].

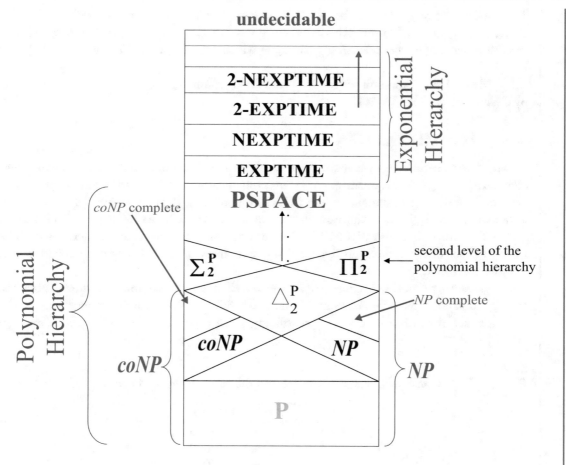

Figure 5.2: Above the polynomial hierarchy.

The idea of the reduction is as follows: Given χ as above, the empty instance D of schema $\mathcal{S} \cup \{P(\cdot), U_1(\cdot), \ldots, U_n(\cdot)\}$, with universe $U_n = \{a_1, \ldots, a_n, a\}$, is considered.

The integrity constraint φ is:

$$\bigwedge_{i=1}^{n} \forall x \forall y \, (U_i(x) \wedge U_i(y) \to x = y) \wedge \bigwedge_{i=1}^{n} \bigvee_{j=1}^{n} U_i(a_j) \, \wedge$$

$$\forall x_1 \cdots \forall x_n (\bigwedge_{i=1}^{n} U_i(x_i) \to \forall \bar{y} \, \psi(x_1, \ldots, x_n, \bar{y})) \, \vee \, P(a).$$

The BSC-sentence χ is satisfiable iff $D \not\models_{\{\varphi\}} P(a)$. That φ is a safe universal IC depends on $\psi(x_1, \ldots, x_n, \bar{y})$ only. However, this issue can be addressed by using a "safe" subclass of BSC, namely formulas encoding the *bounded tiling problem*, for which SAT is also $NEXP$-complete [Börger et al., 2001].

Many issues are still open wrt combined complexity of CQA; they are discussed by Arenas and Bertossi [2010].

5.6   AGGREGATION

So far, only first-order queries have been considered. It is natural to ask about algorithms and complexity of CQA for aggregate queries. This problem was first addressed by Arenas et al. [2003b], for atomic scalar aggregate queries and FDs. More precisely, the queries use only one element of a standard set of SQL scalar aggregation operators, namely: MIN, MAX, COUNT(*), COUNT(A), SUM, and AVG. However, queries with GROUP BY were not considered. The repair semantics is the "classic" tuple- and set-oriented one; and the conflict-graph representation of repairs described in Section 3.3 was heavily used.

However, the notion of consistent answer was changed, to accommodate numerical values and the high likelihood that different repairs would lead to different values for the aggregations, producing an empty set of consistent answers. Accordingly, a *range semantics* was introduced [Arenas et al., 2003b].

Example 5.1   Consider a database instance and the *FD*: *Name* → *Amount*.

Salary	Name	Amount
	smith	5000
	smith	8000
	jones	3000
	stone	7000

The repairs are:

Salary	Name	Amount
	smith	5000
	jones	3000
	stone	7000

Salary	Name	Amount
	smith	8000
	jones	3000
	stone	7000

If the query is Q_1: MIN(Amount), and we use the original notion of consistent answer, we would get 3000 as a consistent answer, because MIN(Amount) returns 3000 in every repair.

However, for the query Q_2: MAX(Amount), the maximum, 8000, comes from a tuple that participates in the violation of *FD*. Actually, MAX(Amount) returns a different value in each repair: 7000 and 8000, resp. There is no consistent answer as originally defined. ∎

Definition 5.2   [Arenas et al., 2003b] The *consistent answer to an aggregate query* Q from the database instance D is the shortest numerical interval that contains all the answers $Q(D')$ to Q obtained from the repairs D' of D.   ∎

Graphically:

$$Q(D')$$

min-answers to Q a b *max-answers to* Q

$$- - - - \ | \ - - - - - - - - - \ | \ - - - -$$

for all repairs D'

A *min-answer* is any numerical value k such that, for every repair D', the value $aggr(D')$ of the aggregate query in D' satisfies $k \leq aggr(D')$. Similarly, for a *max-answer* k, $aggr(D') \leq k$ holds for every repair D'. The main problem becomes determining the optimum bounds a and b: a is called the *max-min answer*, and b, the *min-max answer*, denoted max-$min(aggr, D)$ and min-$max(aggr, D)$, resp. In Example 5.1, max-$min(\texttt{MAX(Amount)}, D) = 7000$ and min-$max(\texttt{MAX(Amount)}, D) = 8000$, resp., and the (optimal) interval [7000, 8000] is the consistent answer to the query MAX(Amount). (This range semantics has also been applied in the context of data exchange with aggregate queries [Afrati and Kolaities, 2008].)

Now the problem becomes developing algorithms for the optimization problems of computing the *max-min answer*, a (a minimization problem in the class of repairs); and/or the *min-max answer*, b (a maximization problem). Hopefully, without explicitly computing the repairs, but querying the original instance D. Determining the complexity of computing each of these optimum bounds also becomes a natural problem. These are the decision versions of the optimization problems. They are, respectively: (a) deciding if max-$min(aggr, D) \leq k$, i.e., if there exists a repair D' with $aggr(D') \leq k$; and (b) deciding if min-$max(aggr, D) \geq k$, i.e., if there exists a repair D' with $aggr(D') \geq k$.

For example, MAX(A) can be different in every repair, but the maximum of the MAX(A)'s, b, is MAX(A) in D. So, computing the min-max answer to MAX(A) from D is immediate. Now, computing directly from D the minimum of the MAX(A)'s, i.e., the max-min answer, a, to MAX(A), does not look that direct. However, computing the max-min answer to MAX(A) *for one FD F* is in *PTIME* (in data).

The following is an algorithm that computes the max-min answer to MAX(A) for an instance D of a schema $R(X, Y)$ with the FD: $X \rightarrow Y$. It is a query rewriting algorithm that uses the following sequence of SQL queries to the inconsistent database:

1. For each group of (X, Y)-values, store the maximum of A:
   ```
   CREATE VIEW S(X,Y,C) AS
   SELECT X,Y,MAX(A) FROM R
   GROUP BY X,Y;
   ```
2. For each value of X, store the minimum of the maxima:
   ```
   CREATE VIEW T(X,C) AS
   SELECT X, MIN(C) FROM S
   GROUP BY X;
   ```

3. Output the maximum of the minima:
   ```
   SELECT MAX(C) FROM T;
   ```

This sequence of queries can be computed in polynomial time on D. Repairs are not explicitly computed. The rewriting of the original query still uses SQL with aggregation, but it uses GROUP BY.

Now, adding one FD may change the complexity. Actually, with more than one FD, the problem of deciding whether the max-min answer to MAX(A) $\leq k$ is *NP*-complete [Arenas et al., 2003b].

NP-hardness is obtained by reduction from propositional *SAT*. The idea is as follows: For a propositional formula φ in CNF of the form $C_1 \wedge \cdots \wedge C_n$, with propositional variables $p_1, \ldots p_m$, build a database D with attributes X, Y, Z, W, and the following tuples:

1. $(p_i, 1, C_j, 1)$ if making p_i true makes C_j true;

2. $(p_i, 0, C_j, 1)$ if making p_i false makes C_j true;

3. $(w, w, C_j, 2), 1 \leq j \leq n$, with w a new symbol.

Consider the following set *FD* of FDs: $X \to Y$, expressing that each propositional variable cannot have more than one truth value, and also $Z \to W$. It holds that φ is satisfiable iff for D, *FD*, and $k = 1$, the answer to our decision instance is *Yes*.

Just to mention another complexity result, even for one FD, the problem of deciding if the max-min-answer to COUNT(A) $\leq k$ is *NP*-complete. Several results of this kind are presented in [Arenas et al., 2003b]. The table in Figure 5.3 summarizes the complexity results for the different scalar aggregate queries, depending on the number of FDs.

	max-min-answer		min-max-answer	
	$\|FD\| = 1$	$\|FD\| \geq 2$	$\|FD\| = 1$	$\|FD\| \geq 2$
MIN(A)	*PTIME*	*PTIME*	*PTIME*	*NP*-complete
MAX(A)	*PTIME*	*NP*-complete	*PTIME*	*PTIME*
COUNT(*)	*PTIME*	*NP*-complete	*PTIME*	*NP*-complete
COUNT(A)	*NP*-complete	*NP*-complete	*NP*-complete	*NP*-complete
SUM(A)	*PTIME*	*NP*-complete	*PTIME*	*NP*-complete
AVG(A)	*PTIME*	*NP*-complete	*PTIME*	*NP*-complete

Figure 5.3: Complexity results for scalar aggregate queries.

Some normalization conditions, e.g., BCNF, have been identified under which, in some cases, more efficient algorithms can be obtained. Similar improvements are possible when certain conditions on the conflict hold, e.g., being *claw-free* [Arenas et al., 2003b].

Consistently answering aggregate queries under the range semantics was retaken as an extension of the work on conjunctive queries and their classification in terms of the class

$\mathcal{C}_{Tree}$ [Fuxman et al., 2005] (cf. Section 3.4). Group-by was considered. Additional complexity results on consistent answering of queries with aggregation are obtained in [Bertossi et al., 2008, Sec. 6]. Still the range semantics is used, but the repairs are attribute-based (cf. Sections 2.5.6 and 5.8.1.1).

A different research direction emerges with aggregation appearing in the ICs, obtaining *aggregation constraints*. For example, the aggregation constraint,

$$\text{SUM}(A_1 : A_2 < 3) > 100, \tag{5.6}$$

requires that the sum of the values of attribute A_1 in the tuples where attribute A_3 takes a value smaller than 3 has to be greater than 100. Under the attribute-based repair semantics of numerical databases under denial constraints, deciding the existence of repairs becomes undecidable [Bertossi et al., 2008, Sec. 7.3].

A more systematic investigation of attribute-based repairs and consistent query answering under aggregation constraints is provided by Flesca et al. [2010a] (cf. Section 5.8.2).

5.7 CARDINALITY-BASED REPAIRS

With a few exceptions, most of the research on CQA has used the tuple- and set-oriented repair semantics for relational databases (cf. Section 2.5.1). Among the exceptions, we find two alternative repair semantics for which some results have been obtained. One is the *cardinality-based repair semantics* (cf. Section 2.5.5) that we consider here. The other is the *attribute-based repair semantics* (cf. Section 2.5.6), which we describe in Section 5.8.

A cardinality-based repair, *C-repair* in short, of an instance D is a tuple-oriented repair D' that minimizes the cardinality $|\Delta(D, D')|$ [Arenas et al., 2003a].

Example 5.3 For the schema $P(X, Y, Z)$, with $FD: X \rightarrow Y$, the instance $D = \{P(a, b, c), P(a, c, d), P(a, c, e)\}$ has two repairs wrt set inclusion, i.e., that minimize $\Delta(D, D')$ wrt set inclusion:

1. $D_1 = \{P(a, b, c)\}$, with $\Delta(D, D_1) = \{P(a, c, d), P(a, c, e)\}$.

2. $D_2 = \{P(a, c, d), P(a, c, e)\}$, with $\Delta(D, D_2) = \{P(a, b, c)\}$.

Only D_2 is a C-repair: $|\Delta(D, D_2)|$ is minimum. ∎

Remark 5.4 In the next two sections we will be sometimes making comparisons between different kinds of repairs (or, more precisely, repair semantics). To ease this comparison, we will refer to them using the following short forms:

S-repairs: Repairs based on minimal set difference.

C-repairs: Repairs based on minimum cardinality set difference.

A-repairs: Repairs obtained through changes of attribute values and based on some sort of minimization of those changes (cf. Section 5.8). ∎

The repair semantics of choice may depend on the application domain and databases at hand. For example, the C-repair semantics may be better when a few tuples are in conflict with many others. Also, the general properties of a repair semantics may be considered. For example, C-repairs are a subset of S-repairs, so more consistent answers can be obtained.

The same computational problem can be considered according to a particular repair semantics, say $\mathfrak{S}$. For example, if $Rep(D, IC, \mathfrak{S})$ denotes the class of repairs of D wrt IC, and the repair semantics $\mathfrak{S}$, we could consider the decision problem

$$CQA(Q, IC, \mathfrak{S}) := \{ D \mid D' \models Q \text{ for all } D' \in Rep(D, IC, \mathfrak{S}) \} .$$

Lopatenko and Bertossi [2007] undertake the first systematic analysis of C-repairs, and provide complexity results. Some of these are discussed in the rest of this section.

We concentrate mostly on denial ICs, which include functional dependencies. In consequence, C-repairs are obtained by tuple deletions only; and the class formed by them can be represented by means of a *conflict-hypergraph* (cf. Section 3.3). More precisely, there is a one-to-one correspondence between C-repairs of D wrt IC and the maximum independent sets of $\mathcal{HG}(D, IC)$, i.e., independent sets of maximum cardinality (MIS). Here, an independent set in a hypergraph is a set of vertices that does not contain any hyperedge.

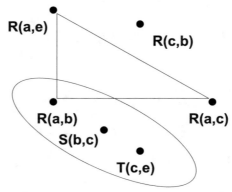

Figure 5.4: A conflict-hypergraph.

Example   5.5   For   the   set $IC = \{\forall xyz \neg (R(x, y) \land R(x, z) \land y \neq z), \forall xyzw \neg (R(x, y) \land S(y, z) \land T(z, w))\}$, and the instance $D = \{R(a, b), R(a, c), R(a, e), R(c, b), S(b, c), T(c, e)\}$, we have the conflict-hypergraph in Figure 5.4. ∎

More generally, it is easy to verify that the following hold.

(a) A ground atomic query is consistently true if it is a vertex in every MIS. This is the usual "certain" semantics for CQA.

(b) Every tuple in D belongs to an S-repair, but not necessarily to a C-repair.

In consequence, testing membership of vertices to some MIS (the "possible" semantics for CQA) becomes relevant. For these two problems, we have the following useful polynomial-time self-reducibility properties for MIS: (the reductions should be clear from the corresponding figures)

(A) For every $v \in \mathcal{G}$: $v \in$ some MIS of $\mathcal{G}$ iff $v \in$ all MIS of $\mathcal{G}'$ iff $|MIS|(\mathcal{G})$ and $|MIS|(\mathcal{G}')$ differ by one. Here, $|MIS|(\mathcal{G})$ denotes the size of a MIS of $\mathcal{G}$.

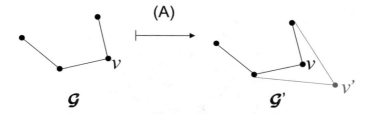

Figure 5.5: Reduction from possible to certain semantics.

(B) For every $v \in \mathcal{G}$: $v \in$ all MIS of $\mathcal{G}$ iff $v \in$ some MIS of $\mathcal{G}'$.

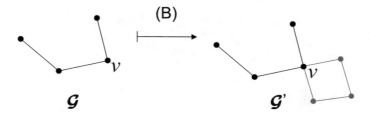

Figure 5.6: Reduction from certain to possible semantics.

We are formulating the results in terms of (conflict) graphs, but they carry over to (conflict) hypergraphs. As a consequence, of these general results we obtain that: *The problems of CQA under the certain and the possible C-repair semantics are polynomially reducible to each other.* This is not necessarily true for the S-repair semantics.

With this result it is possible to bundle together the two problems in terms of their complexity. Actually, it holds that *the problems of deciding for a vertex in a graph if it belongs to some MIS and if it belongs to all MISs are both in* $P^{NP(log(n))}$ (the class of problems that can be solved in polynomial time with a logarithmic number of calls to an *NP* oracle). This result is obtained by using as a subroutine an algorithm for computing the size of a maximum clique in a graph, which belongs to $FP^{NP(log(n))}$ [Krentel, 1988]. (The F in the complexity class name stands for "functional" problems, i.e., about function computation, as opposed to decision problems.) As a consequence, we can conclude that: *For denial constraints and ground atomic queries, CQA under the C-repair semantics belongs to* $P^{NP(log(n))}$.

In order to obtain a hardness result, we can make good use of a *a representation lemma*: There is a fixed database schema $\mathcal{S}$ and a denial constraint, such that for every graph $\mathcal{G}$, there is an instance D for $\mathcal{S}$, whose C-repairs are in one-to-one correspondence with the MISs of $\mathcal{G}$. Actually, D can be built in polynomial time in the size of $\mathcal{G}$ [Lopatenko and Bertossi, 2007, Lemma 4].

For hardness, we establish first an auxiliary polynomial-time graph construction, associated to a given graph $\mathcal{G}$, *the block* $B_k(\mathcal{G}, \mathbf{t})$, with $k \in \mathbb{N}$, that is shown in Figure 5.7.

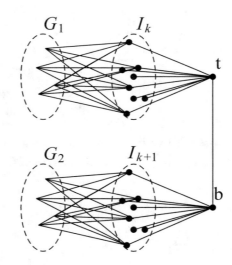

Figure 5.7: The block $B_k(\mathcal{G}, \mathbf{t})$.

$B_k(\mathcal{G}, \mathbf{t})$ is built as follows:

1. G_1, G_2 are copies of the given graph $\mathcal{G}$.

2. $\mathbf{t}$ is a distinguished vertex.

3. Two internally disconnected subgraphs I_k, I_{k+1}, with k and $k + 1$ nodes, resp.

4. Every vertex in G_1 (G_2) is connected to every vertex in I_k (I_{k+1}).

By construction, it holds that the cardinality of an MIS of $\mathcal{G}$ is equal to k iff $\mathbf{t}$ belongs to all MISs of $B_k(\mathcal{G}, \mathbf{t})$. This construction and property allow us to obtain the following.

Proposition 5.6 [Lopatenko and Bertossi, 2007] Deciding if a vertex belongs to all MISs of a graph $\mathcal{G}$ is $P^{NP(log(n))}$-hard. ∎

The proof is by reduction from the following $P^{NP(log(n))}$-complete problem [Krentel, 1988]: Given a graph $\mathcal{G}$ and an integer k, is the size of a maximum clique in $\mathcal{G}$ equivalent to 0 *mod* k?

The reduction takes the complement graph of $\mathcal{G}$ and creates a graph $\mathcal{G}'$ that is a combination of a number of versions of the block construction, so that counting sizes of maximum independent sets can be represented.

By the representation lemma mentioned above, the graph in Proposition 5.6 can be represented as (or reduced to) a database consistency problem. In this way we obtain the main result: *For denial constraints, CQA for ground atomic queries under the C-repair semantics is $P^{NP(log(n))}$-complete* [Lopatenko and Bertossi, 2007].

We should contrast this result with the one for the S-repair semantics already mentioned in Section 5.2: The very same problem can be solved in polynomial time. And for conjunctive boolean queries and denial ICs, CQA is *coNP*-complete [Chomicki and Marcinkowski, 2005]. In contrast to the S-repair semantics, the C-repair semantics also has a higher complexity repair checking problem, namely *coNP*-complete vs. *PTIME*. Afrati and Kolaitis [2009] provide additional results on repair checking under the C-repair semantics. We will see in Section 5.9 that, on the other side, the C-repairs behave better in a dynamic scenario.

To finalize this section, we should mention that C-repairs can be captured as models of disjunctive logic programs with stable model semantics. The programs are basically as those used to represent S-repairs (cf. Section 4.1). However, *weak program constraints* have to be used [Arenas et al., 2003a, Sec. 8]. They can be minimally violated by the stable models of the program, as opposed to (hard) program constraints that have to be fully satisfied, like those in 5. in Example 4.2. This gives us an immediate upper-bound of $\Delta_3^P(log(n))$ in data complexity for CQA [Buccafurri et al., 2000].

5.8 ATTRIBUTE-BASED REPAIRS

The attribute-based repair semantics, or A-repair semantics (cf. Remark 5.4), comes in different forms depending on how attribute-values are changed and how a general distance measure between instances is defined. Usually, the number of changes is minimized, but the distance function may be more general. The distance usually depends on some aggregate numerical function, specially if the attribute-values are numerical themselves. Actually, the latter is the case we describe in more detail in this section (cf. Section 5.8.1). Cf. Section 5.9 for some additional, general results on CQA under the A-repair semantics, e.g., Proposition 5.15.

A-repairs are natural in some scenarios, e.g., with census-like data. There, new and different ontological assumptions, data fixes[2], and computational needs appear in comparison with traditional data management [Franconi et al., 2001]. For example:[3]

(a) Many attributes take numerical values.

(b) The most natural form of fix is to change some of the values of attributes in tuples.

(c) The tuples are identified by a key, e.g., a household identifier, that is fixed and not subject to changes. The identifiers are kept in any repaired version of the database (or census form).

(d) Constraints are expressed as prohibitions on combined positive data.

(e) We find few relations in the database. Actually, it is not uncommon to have one single relation.

(f) Most importantly, the *computation of fixes (repairs) becomes crucial*. In census applications this is a common, *editing*, task. The repairs become important *per se*, possibly more than consistent answers.

(g) Aggregate queries become most important, rather than queries about individual properties.

Franconi et al. [2001] specify attribute-based repairs by means of logic programs with stable model semantics. Different changes of attribute values are considered and generated when a denial constraint, that prohibits certain combinations of values in a census form (e.g., being 5 years old and married), is violated. The minimization of the number of changes is enforced by means of weak program constraints, to filter out all stable models where the number of changes is not minimum [Buccafurri et al., 2000].

Bohannon et al. [2005] investigate attribute-based repairs for violations of FDs and (not necessarily full) inclusion dependencies. FD violations are solved by changes of attribute values; whereas inclusion dependencies, by tuple insertions. Tuples have weights that reflect the confidence in them or the cost of changing values in them. Actually, the real cost of such a change is multiplied by the distance between the old and the new value. Inserting a tuple into a table has a fixed cost associated to the table. With all these elements, a (minimal) repair of an instance D is a new instance that does satisfy the ICs and has a minimum cost.

As we can see, the repairs in [Bohannon et al., 2005] are A-repairs on the FD side. Still on that side, what is minimized is an aggregation function over triples $\langle R(\bar{t}), A, v \rangle$ (indicating that the original value for attribute A in tuple $\bar{t}$ of table R was changed to value v). This function rather complex in comparison to the sheer counting of changes.

Much motivated by data cleaning, actually also bringing several data cleaning elements into the repair framework, the emphasis in [Bohannon et al., 2005] is on computing a minimal repair

---

[2]Repairs were called *fixes* in (the previous conference version of) Wijsen [2005]. They were obtained by via database (value) updates. In this Section, we keep this term, to distinguish them from tuple-oriented repairs.

[3]Cf. United Nations Economic Commission for Europe, Work Session on Statistical Data Editing (Ottawa, May 16-18, 2005): http://www.unece.org/stats/documents/2005.05.sde.htm

(as opposed to CQA). The problem of deciding if there is a repair for an instance D with cost not greater than a budget C turns out to be NP-complete (in the size of D). This results holds for a fixed set of FDs, and separately, for a fixed set of inclusion dependencies [Bohannon et al., 2005]. On the basis of this results, the authors present an efficient approximation algorithm.

5.8.1   DENIAL CONSTRAINTS AND NUMERICAL DOMAINS

Bertossi et al. [2008] study A-repairs that minimize a numerical aggregation function over differences between numerical attribute values in the original tuples and in their repaired versions. Additional assumptions, or elements of this framework, are the following:

(a) The schemas have key constraints that are always satisfied, i.e., they are *hard constraints*.

(b) Only some numerical attributes may take erroneous values.

(c) The ICs that can be violated, i.e., *soft constraints*, are denial constraints; they prohibit certain combinations of data values.

(d) Only changes of values in fixable numerical, actually integer, attributes are allowed to restore consistency.

(e) A quadratic distance is kept to a minimum.

Example 5.7   [Bertossi et al., 2008] Consider the following denial constraints and an inconsistent database instance, D:

$$IC_1: \forall ID, P, A, M \neg (Buy(ID, I, P), Client(ID, A, M), A < 18, P > 25),$$
$$IC_2: \forall ID, A, M \neg (Client(ID, A, M), A < 18, M > 50).$$

D:

Client	ID	A	M
	1	15	52
	2	16	51
	3	60	900
Buy	**ID**	**I**	**P**
	1	CD	27
	1	DVD	26
	3	DVD	40

The denial constraints tell us that: *People younger than 18 cannot spend more than 25 on one item nor spend more than 50 in the store.*

In order to restore consistency, values for attributes **A**, **M**, and **P** can be changed, in such a way the the sum of the squares of the differences between old and new values is minimized. In this case, a (minimal) repair is D' with $cost = 1^2 + 2^2 + 1^2 + 2^2 = 10$. Another (minimal) repair is D'',

D'

Client	ID	A	M
	1	15	~~52~~ 50
	2	16	~~51~~ 50
	3	60	900
Buy	ID	I	P
	1	CD	~~27~~ 25
	1	DVD	~~26~~ 25
	3	DVD	40

D''

Client	ID	A	M
	1	~~15~~ 18	52
	2	16	~~51~~ 50
	3	60	900
Buy	ID	I	P
	1	CD	27
	1	DVD	26
	3	DVD	40

Figure 5.8: Two minimal fixes.

also with $cost = 1^2 + 3^2 = 10$. They are shown in Figure 5.8. Notice that the key constraints are satisfied in all of D, D', D''. ∎

In the rest of this section we describe results obtained in [Bertossi et al., 2008] for the class of *linear denial constraints* (LDCs), i.e., those of the form $\forall \bar{x} \neg (A_1 \wedge \ldots \wedge A_m)$, where A_i are database atoms, or built-in atoms of the form $X \theta c$, with $\theta \in \{=, \neq, <, >, \leq, \geq\}$, or $X = Y$ (the latter can be replaced by different occurrences of the same variable). When they contain atoms of the form $X \neq Y$, they are called *extended linear denial constraints* (ELDs).

In order to introduce a distance function between instances, we impose the condition that, when numerical values are updated to restore consistency, the smallest overall variation of the original values must be achieved. These variations can be computed, because a database and a fix share the same key values. In consequence, key values can be used to compute associated numerical variations.

More precisely, to compare instances, we need a common relational schema $\mathcal{R}$, a set of key constraints $\mathcal{K}$, assumed to be satisfied by all the instances, the set of attributes $\mathcal{A}$, and a subset of *fixable, integer attributes* $\mathcal{F}$ that does not contain any attributes in the key. A combination of key values can be used as a tuple identifier. That is, for a tuple $\bar{k}$ of key values in relation R in instance D, $\bar{t}(\bar{k}, R, D)$ denotes the unique tuple $\bar{t}$ in relation R in D whose key value is $\bar{k}$.

Example 5.8   (Example 5.7 continued) We have the following relational predicates $Client(\underline{ID}, A, M)$ and $Buy(\underline{ID, I}, P)$, with their key underlined. Here, $\mathcal{F} = \{A, M, P\}$. For example, $\bar{t}((1, CD), Buy, D) = Buy(1, CD, 27)$, etc. ∎

For instances D, D' over the same schema and same key values for each predicate $R \in \mathcal{R}$, their *square distance* is

$$d(D, D') = \sum \alpha_A [\pi_A(\bar{t}(\bar{k}, R, D)) - \pi_A(\bar{t}(\bar{k}, R, D'))]^2,$$

where the sum is over all predicates R, fixable numerical attributes $A \in \mathcal{F}$, and tuples of key values $\bar{k}$. Here, π_A denotes the projection on attribute A, and α_A is the application-dependent *weight* of attribute A. Other numerical distance functions can be considered, obtaining results similar to those described below [Bertossi et al., 2008].

Given an instance D, with $D \models \mathcal{K}$, and a set of possibly violated ELDCs IC, a *least–squares fix* (LS-fix) for D wrt IC is an instance D', such that:

(a) it has the same schema and domain as D;

(b) it has the same values as D in the non-fixable attributes $\mathcal{A} \smallsetminus \mathcal{F}$ (in particular in key attributes);

(c) $D' \models \mathcal{K} \cup IC$;

(d) $d(D, D')$ is minimum over all the instances that satisfy (a) - (c).

If we require just conditions (a)-(c), we say that D' is a *fix* of D.

For a given set IC and a given instance D, we define:

$$\begin{aligned} LS\text{-}Fix(D, IC) \ &:= \ \{D' \mid D' \text{ is an LS-fix of } D \text{ wrt } IC\}, \\ Fix(D, IC) \ &:= \ \{D' \mid D' \text{ is a fix of } D \text{ wrt } IC\}. \end{aligned}$$

Of course, if D has fixes, it also has LS-fixes, which makes us concentrate mostly on fixes rather than LS-fixes.

As indicated above, in this scenario new issues and problems appear, not considered in previous sections. For example, in contrast to the "classical" case of CQA, there may be no fixes. So, determining the existence of fixes becomes relevant. Other related problems gain prominence, like the *repair checking problem*, computing database fixes, determining the existence of fixes within a certain distance from the original instance; consistent query answering to aggregate queries.

For a fixed set IC of ELDCs, $NE(IC) := \{D \mid Fix(D, IC) \neq \emptyset\}$, the problem of existence of fixes, is *NP*-complete [Bertossi et al., 2008]. However, the most interesting problem is *the database fix problem*:

$$DFP(IC) := \{(D, k) \mid k \in \mathbb{N} \text{ and there is } D' \in Fix(D, IC) \text{ with } d(D, D') \leq k\}. \qquad (5.7)$$

This problem is important for the transformation of an inconsistent database into the closest consistent state, which involves asking about the distance to the closest consistent state. Also, computations are made more efficient by cutting off incorrect (or too expensive) branches during computation or materialization of a consistent state. The *DFP* problem turns out to be *NP*-complete [Bertossi et al., 2008]. The membership of *NP* is obtained from the fact that the possible values in repaired tuples are determined by the constants in the ELDCs, and the computation of the distance function is in *PTIME*. Hardness can be obtained by reduction from the *Vertex Cover* problem. Actually, one LDC with three database atoms plus two built-ins is good enough for this.

Considering this result and the relevance of computing a good fix in this kind of applications, it is natural to ask about the possibility of obtaining an efficient approximate solution. To investigate this problem, it is natural to refer to an associated optimization problem: *DFOP* denotes the optimization problem of finding the minimum distance to a fix. In this regard, it is possible to prove that, for a fixed set of LDCs, *DFOP* is *MAXSNP*-hard [Bertossi et al., 2008]. The proof is by reduction from *Minimum Vertex Cover for Graphs of Bounded Degree*, which is *MAXSNP*-complete. The *MAXSNP*-hardness property implies (unless *P=NP*) that there exists a constant δ such that *DFOP* for LDCs cannot be efficiently approximated within an approximation factor less than δ [Papadimitriou, 1994].

The next question is about the existence of efficient approximations within an arbitrarily small constant factor, for a restricted, hard, and still interesting class of LDCs. Example 5.7 hints at such a class.

Example 5.9 (Example 5.7 continued) We will introduce names for the tuples in the database. They are shown in an extra column in each table. In the initial instance D:

Client	ID	A	M	
	1	15	52	t_1
	2	16	51	t_2
	3	60	900	t_3

Buy	ID	I	P	
	1	CD	27	t_4
	1	DVD	26	t_5
	3	DVD	40	t_6

IC_1 is violated by $\{t_1, t_4\}$ and $\{t_1, t_5\}$; IC_2 by $\{t_1\}$ and $\{t_2\}$. Assuming that $\alpha_A = \alpha_M = \alpha_P = 1$, we find the two LS-fixes, D' and D'', we had before:

Client	ID	A	M	
	1	15	5̶2̶ 50	t_1'
	2	16	5̶1̶ 50	t_2'
	3	60	900	t_3

Buy	ID	I	P	
	1	CD	2̶7̶ 25	t_4'
	1	DVD	2̶6̶ 25	t_5'
	3	DVD	40	t_6

Client	ID	A	M	
	1	1̶5̶ 18	52	t_1''
	2	16	5̶1̶ 50	t_2''
	3	60	900	t_3

Buy	ID	I	P	
	1	CD	27	t_4
	1	DVD	26	t_5
	3	DVD	40	t_6

In this case, it was possible to obtain LS-fixes by performing direct, *local changes* in the original conflictive tuples alone. No new, intermediate inconsistencies are introduced in the repair process. For other classes of LDCs this might not be always the case. ∎

A set of LDCs *IC* is *local* if: (a) equalities between attributes and joins involve only non-fixable attributes; (b) there is a built-in with a fixable attribute in each IC; (c) no attribute A appears in IC both in comparisons of the form $A < c_1$ and $A > c_2$ [Bertossi et al., 2008]. For example, the set of LDCs in Example 5.7 is local.

Local sets of LDCs are interesting, because inconsistencies can be fixed tuple by tuple, without introducing new violations; and LS-fixes always exist. Furthermore, local LDCs are the most common in census-like applications [Franconi et al., 2001].

It can be proved that *DFP* is still *NP*-complete and *MAXSNP*-hard for local LDCs [Bertossi et al., 2008]. However, it is still possible to provide a useful efficient approximation to *DFP* for local sets of LDCs. This can be done by reduction of *DFOP*, the associated optimization problem, to the *Weighted Set Cover Problem* (*WSCP*).

The *WSCP* is as follows. First, an instance is of the form $(U, \mathcal{S}, w)$, where $\mathcal{S}$ is a collection of subsets of set U with $\bigcup \mathcal{S} = U$; and w assigns numerical weights to elements of $\mathcal{S}$. The problem is to find a sub-collection of $\mathcal{S}$ with minimum weight that still covers U. It is known that *WSCP* is also *MAXSNP*-hard. However, starting from the *DFOP* problem, it is possible to produce a "good" instance of *WSCP*, as follows.

1. A set I of database atoms (tuples) from D is a violation set for $ic \in IC$ if $I \not\models ic$, and for every $I' \subsetneq I$, $I' \models ic$, i.e., a minimal set of tuples that participate in the violation of an IC. Next, the basic set for the *WSCP* is defined by $U :=$ set of violation sets for D, IC.

2. $\mathcal{I}(D, ic, t)$ denotes the set of violation sets for ic in D that contain tuple t. Now, we consider $S(t, t') := \{I \mid \text{exists } ic \in IC, \ I \in \mathcal{I}(D, ic, t) \text{ and } ((I \smallsetminus \{t\}) \cup \{t'\}) \models ic\}$. These are the violations sets containing tuple t that are solved by changing t to t'. Next, the cover for U becomes $\mathcal{S} :=$ collection of $S(t, t')$'s such that t' is a *local fix* of t, i.e., (a) t, t' share same values in non-fixable attributes; (b) $S(t, t') \neq \emptyset$ (some inconsistency is solved); (c) $d(\{t\}, \{t'\})$ is minimum (relative to (a) and (b)).

3. Finally, the last element of the *WSCP* is $w(S(t, t')) := d(\{t\}, \{t'\})$.

This reduction has some interesting properties: (a) local fixes and the whole reduction can be done in polynomial time; (b) there is a one-to-one correspondence between solutions to *DFOP* and solutions to the associated *WSCP* that keeps the optimum values; (c) each set cover corresponds to a consistent instance. It is interesting to indicate that the correspondence may be lost when applied to non-local sets of LDCs.

Example 5.10   (Example 5.7 continued) The violation sets associated to instance D are shown in the figure: $\{t_1, t_4\}$, $\{t_1, t_5\}$ for IC_1; and $\{t_1\}$, $\{t_2\}$ for IC_2. (Notice the similarity with the conflict hypergraphs of Section 3.3.)

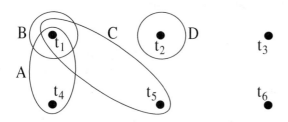

Client	ID	A	M	
	1	15	52	t_1
	2	16	51	t_2
	3	60	900	t_3
Buy	ID	I	P	
	1	CD	27	t_4
	1	DVD	26	t_5
	3	DVD	40	t_6

Tuple t_1 has one local fix wrt IC_1, and one wrt IC_2. Tuple t_2 has one local fix, and tuples t_4, t_5 have one local fix each. The tuples, their local fixes, and weights are shown in the following table:

Set cover els.	$S(t_1, t_1')$	$S(t_1, t_1'')$	$S(t_2, t_2')$	$S(t_4, t_4')$	$S(t_5, t_5')$
Local Fix	t_1'	t_1''	t_2'	t_4'	t_5'
Weight	4	9	1	4	1
Violation set A	0	1	0	1	0
Violation set B	1	1	0	0	0
Violation set C	0	1	0	0	1
Violation set D	0	0	1	0	0

Here, the values 1 or 0 associated to a violation sets indicate if the latter belongs or not to $S(t, t')$. ∎

An approximation to *DFOP* can be obtained by approximating the associated *WSCP*. In general, *WSCP* can be approximated within a factor $O(log(n))$ using a greedy algorithm [Chvatal, 1979]. However, in our case, the frequency (i.e., the number of elements of S covering an element of U) is bounded by the maximum number of atoms in the LDCs (which is usually small). Under these conditions, *WSCP* can be efficiently approximated within a constant factor given by the maximum frequency [Hochbaum, 1997]. Actually, the approximation algorithm always returns a cover, from which it is possible to compute an instance. This instance always satisfy the LDCs, but it may not be optimal. (In Example 5.7, we get D' though.) Details can be found in [Bertossi et al., 2008]. An implementation and experiments with this approximation algorithm have been reported by Lopatenko and Bravo [2003].

5.8.1.1 Attribute-based repairs and CQA

In this section, so far we have concentrated on decision and computational problems related to the existence of a repair. Now, in relation to consistent query answering we also have several computational problems that are decision or optimization problems depending on the (consistent) query answering semantics.

Natural alternatives for a semantics to consider in this kind of applications are the:

(a) *Certain* answers: Answers from every LS-fix (this is the usual and default semantics).

(b) *Possible* answers: Answers from some LS-fix.

(c) *Range* answer: The shortest numerical interval where the answers from all the LS-fixes can be found, as in the case of aggregation (cf. Section 5.6)

The range semantics is natural when we have numerical domains and/or aggregate queries. As we saw in Section 5.6, this semantics gives rise to two optimization problems, those of finding the extremes of the interval.

Several complexity results are reported by Bertossi et al. [2008], and several of them for *1-atom linear denial constraints* (1ALDCs), which have one database atom plus built-ins. For example, $\forall u \forall c_1 \forall c_2 \neg (R(u, c_1, c_2) \wedge c_1 < 1 \wedge c_2 < 1)$. They are a common case in census-like applications. For example, for 1ALDCs, atomic (non-aggregate) ground queries and the certain semantics, CQA falls in *PTIME* (this result can be generalized to a broad class of boolean conjunctive queries). Still under the certain semantics, for arbitrary ELDCs, and atomic non-aggregate queries, CQA becomes P^{NP}-hard, but in Π_2^P.

Now, for aggregate queries, with one of SUM, COUNT DISTINCT, AVERAGE, and the *possible semantics*, we may consider the problem of deciding if the aggregate value satisfies in some LS-fix a comparison to a given constant. It holds that for 1ALDCs and acyclic conjunctive queries the problem becomes *coNP*-hard.

The same *coNP*-hardness result can also be obtained for the range semantics. That the query involved is conjunctive means that the aggregate value is defined via a conjunctive query, e.g., $q(\text{COUNT}(z)) \leftarrow R(u, x, y), S(u, z, x)$, whose body is conjunctive. This is a scalar query (it returns a single number). GROUP BYs can be captured by directly collecting in the head and without aggregation, other variables that appear in the body.

For example, for the range semantics, aggregate acyclic conjunctive queries using COUNT DISTINCT, and 1ALDCs, CQA is *coNP*-complete. This result follows by reduction from *MAX-SAT*, the optimization problem of finding a truth assignment that maximizes the number of satisfied clauses in a propositional formula in CNF; or correspondingly, deciding if there exists an assignment for which the number of clauses satisfied is at least k, a given number. This reduction is briefly described below.

We start with a set P of propositional variables, C is a finite collection of clauses over P, and k a positive integer. For such an instance of *MAX-SAT*, the following database instance can be created, by introducing the following:

1. A relation $Var(\underline{P}, C_1, C_2)$, with tuple $(p, 0, 0)$ for every variable p appearing in C. C_1 and C_2 are *fixable* attributes, taking values 0 or 1 (this range can be enforced with fixed 1ALDCs). There is the indicated hard key-constraint on Var.

2. A *non-fixable* relation $Clause(P, C, S)$, with tuple (p, c, s) for every occurrence of $p \in P$ in clause $c \in C$, s is a truth assignment (giving values 0 or 1) for p that satisfies clause c.

3. The 1AD: $\forall p \forall c_1 \forall c_2 \neg (Var(p, c_1, c_2) \wedge c_1 < 1 \wedge c_2 < 1)$.

Notice that the database schema and the 1ALDC are fixed; only the database instance depends upon the set of clauses. We now consider the also fixed query

$$q(\text{COUNT}(\text{DISTINCT } c)) \leftarrow Var(u, c_1, c_2), Clause(u, c, s), c_1 = s \, ,$$

that is asking for the number of clauses that are satisfied in the instance where it is evaluated (in this case, the fixes). In consequence, the *min-max* value over the class of fixes is the maximum number of clauses that can be simultaneously satisfied. The decision problem to solve on the database side is then: *min-max*(COUNT(DISTINCT C)) $\geq k$ (cf. the discussion right after Definition 5.2).

5.8.2   ATTRIBUTE-BASED REPAIRS AND AGGREGATION CONSTRAINTS

Repairs of databases with special numerical attributes have also been investigated by Flesca et al. [2010a,b]. The integrity constraints considered are *aggregation constraints*, which impose conditions on aggregation of numerical data as captured by aggregate queries of the kind described in Section 5.6. More precisely, the aggregation constraints considered are of the form

$$\forall \bar{x}(\psi(\bar{x}) \ \rightarrow \ \Sigma_{i=1}^{n} c_i \cdot \chi(\bar{y}_i) \leq K), \tag{5.8}$$

where $\psi(\bar{x})$ is a quantifier-free conjunctive query, possibly with constants; the c_i, K are rational coefficients, $\chi(\bar{y}_i)$ is a scalar aggregate SUM-query over a relational attribute, possibly with a condition, like the one in (5.6).

Example 5.11   [Flesca et al., 2010a] In the following table, attribute *Value* is numerical and contains both detailed and aggregate values. The latter are expected to coincide with the addition of the corresponding detailed values. For example, in the third tuple, the "aggr" value (250) should be the same as the sum of the "det" values in the first two tuples (100 and 120).

BalanceSheets	Year	Section	Subsection	Type	Value
	2008	Receipts	cash sales	det	100
	2008	Receipts	receivables	det	120
	2008	Receipts	total cash receipts	aggr	250
	2008	Disbursements	payment of accounts	det	120
	2008	Disbursements	capital expenditure	det	20
	2008	Disbursements	long-term financing	det	80
	2008	Disbursements	total disbursements	aggr	220

That is, the aggregation constraint is (the universal closure of)

$$BalanceSheets(x_1, x_2, x_3, x_4, x_5) \rightarrow \quad \mathrm{SUM}(x_5 : Year = x_1 \wedge Section = x_2 \wedge Type = \text{'det'}) =$$
$$\mathrm{SUM}(x_5 : Year = x_1 \wedge Section = x_2 \wedge Type = \text{'aggr'}),$$

which can be easily represented by a pair of formulas of the form (5.8). The given relation is inconsistent wrt the aggregation constraint.   ∎

Under violations of the aggregation constraints, repairs are obtained by changing numerical attribute values, making a *minimum number of changes*.

Given an instance, D, and a set of aggregation constraints, AC, it is not guaranteed that a repair exists. Actually, deciding that if a repair exists is *NP*-complete (in the size of the given instance). Another natural decision problem is *repair checking*, i.e., given D, AC and an instance D', deciding if D' is a repair of D wrt AC. Repair checking turns out to be *coNP*-complete [Flesca et al., 2010a].

Now, wrt CQA, it holds that deciding if a FO ground atomic query Q is true in all repairs of D wrt AC is $\Delta_2^P[log\ n]$-complete (in the size n of given instance) [Flesca et al., 2010a]. This result can be obtained using complexity results for belief revision [Eiter and Gottlob, 1992]. (Connections between CQA and belief revision/update were already discussed by Arenas et al. [1999, 2003a].)

Flesca et al. [2010b] consider aggregate queries in the above framework. The (consistent) query answer semantics is a *range semantics*, as in [Arenas et al., 2003b]. That is, the consistent answer to a scalar {MIN,MAX, SUM}-aggregate query, possibly with (WHERE) a condition, is the shortest numerical interval whose end points are taken by same repair (not necessarily the same repair), and the answer to the query obtained from any of the repairs falls within the interval (cf. Section 5.6). The consistent answer is the empty interval if there is no repair. Deciding if the consistent answer to a query is contained in a given interval $\Delta_2^P[log\ n]$-complete [Flesca et al., 2010b].

Flesca et al. [2010a,b] put the repairs of an instance wrt a set of aggregation constraints in correspondence with the solutions to a *integer linear programming* problem. This connection is used to establish complexity results and developing algorithms for repair computation and CQA.

5.9 DYNAMIC ASPECTS, FIXED-PARAMETER TRACTABILITY AND COMPARISONS

Lopatenko and Bertossi [2007] investigate some dynamic aspects of repairs and CQA, including a first investigation of fixed-parameter complexity in this scenario. In the rest if this section, we describe some of the results obtained, which include comparative results for all the three (families of) semantics mentioned in Remark 5.4.

The general problem is to study the impact on CQA of the fact that the database instance may have undergone some updates. More precisely, the problem is as follows: *Assuming that the database instance D is already consistent wrt the given set of ICs, before the updates, what is the complexity of CQA from the instance $U(D)$ obtained by applying a finite sequence U of update operations to D?*

This work was initially motivated by the analysis of this form of incremental complexity. C-repairs seemed to have better properties from this point of view. Eventually a more general picture emerged, including the *static* aspects of C-repairs mentioned in Section 5.7.

Example 5.12   Consider the relational predicate $P(X, Y, Z)$ with the *FD*: $X \to Y$. The instance $D_1 = \{P(a, c, d), P(a, c, e)\}$ is consistent.

For the update operation U : $insert(P(a, f, d))$, $U(D_1)$ becomes inconsistent; and the only C-repair of $U(D_1)$ is D_1 itself. Thus, CQA from $U(D_1)$ amounts to classic query answering from D_1.

If we start from the consistent instance $D_2 = \{P(a, c, d)\}$, the same update action U leads to two C-repairs: D_2, but also $\{P(a, f, d)\}$. Now CQA from $U(D_2)$ is different from classic query answering from D_2 since two repairs have to be considered.   ∎

These problems can be made more precise. Actually, they are about *incremental CQA and parameterized complexity*. Given: (a) D, IC, with $D \models IC$, and (b) $U : U_1, \ldots, U_m$, with $m < c \cdot |D|$, and each U_i being an insertion, deletion or change of attribute value, we want to determine *incremental CQA*, i.e., CQA from $U(D)$ wrt *IC*.

This problem has several dimensions: the repair semantics, the kind of ICs, and the kind of update actions in U (e.g., only insertions). Some results for several combinations of these dimensions are known [Lopatenko and Bertossi, 2007]. For example, in contrast to the "static" case:

Proposition 5.13   [Lopatenko and Bertossi, 2007] For the C-repair semantics, first-order boolean queries, and denial constraints, incremental CQA is in *PTIME* in the size of D.   ∎

A natural question is how does the algorithm do in terms of m, the size of the update sequence. Actually, a naive algorithm provides an upper bound of $O(n \times n^m)$, which is exponential in m. The next question is as to whether it is possible to do better, say in time $O(f(m) \times n^c)$. This is a question about *fixed-parameter tractability* [Flum and Grohe, 2006]. More precisely, we consider the decision problem where the special parameter is the update sequence U, or better, its size m:

$$CQA^p(Q, IC, \mathfrak{S}) \quad := \quad \{(D, U) \mid U \text{ is an update sequence, and } Q \text{ is consistently true} \\ \text{in } U(D) \text{ under repair semantics } \mathfrak{S}\}.$$

It is possible to prove that: *Incremental CQA for ground atomic queries and functional dependencies under the C-repair semantics is in FPT, actually in time $O(log(m) \times (1.2852^m + m \cdot n))$* [Lopatenko and Bertossi, 2007].

The algorithm calls a subroutine for *Vertex Cover*, that belongs to *FPT*. One starts with the conflict graph $\mathcal{G}$, which is totally disconnected by the initial consistency assumption. After the update, consisting of m tuples inserted, the conflict graph becomes $\mathcal{G}'$. A subroutine $VC(\mathcal{G}', k)$ decides if there is a vertex cover of size not greater than k (this is in *FPT*). Next, binary search can be used, starting from m with $VC(\mathcal{G}', \_)$, to determine the size of a minimum vertex cover. This is the minimum number of tuples that have to be removed to restore consistency.

Now, a ground atomic query (a vertex $v \in \mathcal{G}'$) is consistently true if it does not belong to any minimum vertex cover. The answer is *yes* iff the sizes of minimum vertex covers for $\mathcal{G}'$ and $\mathcal{G}' \setminus \{v\}$ are the same.

For FDs, conflict graphs are used, but for more general denial constraints (DCs), we find hypergraphs. However, for DCs the membership of *FPT* of incremental CQA still holds. This is based on the observation that: (a) Since the DCs are fixed, the maximum number d of atoms in them is fixed. This bounds the size of the hyperedges. (b) It is possible to use the membership of *FPT* of the *d-Hitting Set*: Finding the size of a minimum hitting set for a hypergraph with hyperedges bounded in size by d [Niedermeier and Rossmanith, 2003].

Notice that parameterized complexity analysis naturally appears, and in many forms, in CQA, both under the static and incremental versions. Several parameters naturally offer themselves, among them: (a) The number of inconsistencies in the database. (b) The degree of inconsistency, i.e., the maximum number of violations per database tuple. (c) The complexity of inconsistency, reflected by the the length of the longest path in the conflict graph or hypergraph, etc. These parameters are practically relevant in many applications, where inconsistencies are "local", as those considered in Section 5.8.

In contrast with the C-repair semantics, for the S-repair semantics (cf. Remark 5.4) it holds: *For boolean conjunctive queries and denial ICs, incremental CQA is coNP-complete* [Lopatenko and Bertossi, 2007]. This result can be obtained by reduction from the static case for the S-repair semantics.

The difference lies in the fact that the cost of a C-repair cannot exceed the size of an update, whereas the cost of an S-repair may be unbounded wrt the size of an update, as the following example shows:

Example 5.14   Consider the schema $\{R(\cdot), S(\cdot)\}$ with the DC $\forall x \forall y \neg(R(x) \wedge S(y))$. The following is a consistent instance: $D = \{R(1), \ldots, R(n)\}$.

After the update $U = insert(S(0))$, the database becomes inconsistent, and the S-repairs are $\{R(1), \ldots, R(n)\}$ and $\{S(0)\}$. Only the former is a C-repair, at a distance 1 from D. The second S-repair is at a distance n. ■

We now consider the A-repair semantics. It may come in different forms. For comparison with the static case wrt incremental CQA, we consider first a quite general, weighted version of the A-repair semantics. Namely, a numerical weight function w on triples of the form $(R(\bar{t}), A, newValue)$, where: (a) $R(\bar{t}) \in D$, (b) A is an attribute of R, and (c) $newValue$ is a new value for A in $R(\bar{t})$.

The *wA-repairs* are consistent instances that minimize an aggregate function g on the values $w(R(\bar{t}), A, newValue)$. Typically, $w(R(\bar{t}), A, newValue)$ is $\delta(R(\bar{t})[A], newValue)$, which returns 1 or 0 depending on the two arguments being different or not; and g is *sum*, i.e., only the number of changes is counted and minimized. As another example, for the case considered in Section 5.8, we have $w(R(\bar{t}), A, newValue)$ given by $(R(\bar{t})[A] - newValue)^2$, and g is *sum*.

In order to be able to compare the complexities of the static vs. the incremental versions of CQA for the A-repair semantics, we have the following result about the former:

Proposition 5.15   [Lopatenko and Bertossi, 2007] Static CQA for ground atomic queries and denial constraints under the weighted A-repair semantics is P^{NP}-complete. ■

This result can be obtained by reduction from the following P^{NP}-complete problem [Krentel, 1988]: *Given a propositional formula $\psi(X_1, \cdots, X_n)$ in 3CNF, decide if the last variable X_n takes the value 1 in the lexicographically maximum satisfying assignment. (The answer is No when ψ is not satisfiable.)*

Now, for the incremental part, still under denial constraints, deletions as update actions are trivial, because they do not introduce any violations.

Proposition 5.16   [Lopatenko and Bertossi, 2007] Incremental CQA for ground atomic queries and denial constraints under the weighted A-repair semantics is P^{NP}-complete. ■

This is obtained by reduction from static CQA for A-repairs as in [Bertossi et al., 2008] (cf. Section 5.8). Here one tuple insertion is good enough for the update part.

Dynamic aspects of CQA have been largely ignored, and more research on incremental properties of- and incremental algorithms for CQA is necessary to make ideas and techniques applicable in database practice.

CHAPTER 6

Repairs and Data Cleaning

Originally, database repairs were introduced with the purpose of characterizing the consistent data in a possibly inconsistent database, as the data that are invariant under the possible repairs [Arenas et al., 1999]. Along the way, repairs got a life of their own, and they started to be investigated independently from the intrinsically consistent data in a database: A repair D' can be seen as a natural and alternative "clean" version of the original instance D. In this case, cleaning means getting rid of semantic violations while staying as close as possible to D.

In Section 5.8, in a concrete scenario, we argued that deciding the existence of repairs, in general, or within a distance of the initial instance, and computing concrete repairs are natural problems to consider. For example, Afrati and Kolaitis [2009] study the problem of repair checking independently from consistent query answering, under different repair semantics. Several recent publications concentrate on the problem of efficiently computing a "good" repair (or a set thereof) as a form of data cleaning (cf. Section 6.2).

The logic programming representation of database repairs is a suitable tool to compute one of the repairs (or all if desired). Every stable model of the program corresponds to a repair. In this case, we would be asking for one solution to the problem of restoring consistency. Notice that (non-stratified) logic programs with stable model semantics have been successfully used to encode NP-complete combinatorial problems [Baral, 2003, Gelfond and Leone, 2002]. Each stable model corresponds to a solution to the problem, e.g., a coloring of a graph with 3 colors if it exists.

The first paper where repairs and data cleaning are explicitly connected is [Bohannon et al., 2005]. The authors use attribute-based repairs to restore consistency wrt FDs (cf. Section 5.8 for more technical details). In some sense they are inspired by the fact that FD violations are commonly due to different ways to refer to the same entity, e.g., *Students*(103, *John Jones*) vs. *Students*(103, *J. Jones*), with the first argument expected to be a key. In consequence, a repair, and also a common data cleaning process know as *entity-resolution* or *record linkage*, should match the names *John Jones* and *J. Jones* (cf. below). They explicitly bring data cleaning techniques in the repair process, with the aim of computing a single repair with a minimum cost or a single approximate repair. The cost of the repair is measured in terms of the cost of changing values in tuples (some may be more trusted than others), and the distances between the original and the new values (e.g., between *J. Jones* and *John Jones* if one of the two names will be kept).

The last few years have seen the emergence of more principled approaches to data cleaning. They are based on *data quality constraints* that declaratively express quality conditions that a database instance has to satisfy [Fan, 2008, Fan et al., 2010]. Some of them, like *conditional dependencies* [Bravo et al., 2007, Fan et al., 2008], are not conceptually very different from traditional semantic integrity constraints. However, they have a clear data cleaning feel, and they have been used as key components of data cleaning processes.

Example 6.1   [Fan, 2008] Consider a database relation subject to the following functional dependencies: $FD_1 : [CC, AC, Phone] \rightarrow [Street, City, Zip]$, and $FD_2 : [CC, AC] \rightarrow [City]$.

CC	AC	Phone	Name	Street	City	Zip
44	131	1234567	mike	mayfield	NYC	EH4 8 LE
44	131	3456789	rick	crichton	NYC	EH4 8LE
01	908	3456789	joe	mtn ave	NYC	07974

The FDs are satisfied by the instance above, but they are global integrity constraints, and may not capture natural data quality requirements, as related to specific data values. Referring to the latter is important in data quality assessment and data cleaning. For example, we could have the following *conditional functional dependency* (CFD):

$$CFD_1 : [CC = 44, Zip] \rightarrow [Street] .$$

This is conditional FD in the sense that the functional dependency of *Street* upon *Zip* applies when the country code takes the value 44.

More generally, conditional dependencies can be created by endowing a set of classical ICs with a *tableau* (or *pattern*) that indicates forced data value associations. For example,

$$CFD_2 : [CC = 44, AC = 131, Phone] \rightarrow [Street, City = `EDI', Zip] .$$

This CFD requires that under the indicated conditions in the antecedent (CC=44, AC = 131), *Street* and *Zip* functionally depend upon *Phone*, and also the city must take the value *EDI*.

Conditional inclusion dependencies have also been considered. For example, this could be one of them:

$$Order(Title, Price, Type = `book') \subseteq Book(Title, Price) .$$

It can be expressed in classical FO predicate logic, as follows: $\forall x \forall y \forall z (Order(x, y, z) \wedge z = `book' \rightarrow Book(x, y))$.   ∎

Database repairs and consistent query answering have been considered in the context of conditional dependencies [Kolahi and Lakshmanan, 2009, 2010] (cf. Section 6.1).

An important and well-studied problem in data cleaning is about detecting tuples that refer to the same real-world entity, and matching them, producing a single, unified representation for that entity. Different names are given to this problem, e.g., entity resolution, duplicate detection, reference reconciliation, data fusion, etc. [Benjelloun et al., 2009, Bleiholder and Naumann, 2008, Elmagarmid et al., 2007]. In relation to this problem, a different class of data quality constraints has been recently introduced and studied. They are the *matching dependencies* (MDs), that express and generalize entity resolution concerns, in a declarative manner [Fan, 2008, Fan et al., 2009].

Matching dependencies are used to express which values should be matched under certain conditions. For example, the following can be an MD for the schema $\{R_1(X, Y), R_2(X, Y)\}$:

$$\forall X_1 X_2 Y_1 Y_2 (R_1[X_1] \approx R_2[X_2] \longrightarrow R_1[Y_1] \doteq R_2[Y_2]).^1$$

It specifies that, when the values for attributes X_1 in R_1 and X_2 in R_2 in two tuples are similar, then the values in those two tuples for attribute Y_1 in R_1 and Y_2 in R_2 must be made equal (matched). Of course, R_1 and R_2 can be same predicate. The similarity relations are domain-dependent, reflexive and symmetric.

Although declarative, MDs have a procedural feel and a "dynamic" semantics. That is, an MD is satisfied by pairs of databases (D, D'): One, D, where the antecedent is satisfied, and a second one, D', where the matching indicated in the consequent is realized [Fan et al., 2009]. Alternative semantics for MDs and computational methods for obtaining clean instances wrt a set of MDs have been proposed by Bertossi et al. [2011] and Gardezi et al. [2011]. The idea is to apply a non-deterministic chase procedure that reaches a *stable instance*, D_n, i.e., one such that the pair (D_n, D_n) satisfies all the MDs. This would be a clean instance. Some comparisons between clean instances wrt MDs and database repairs wrt FDs have been established [Gardezi et al., 2011].

The interaction of classical ICs and database repairs with quality constraints of the kinds considered above has been investigated by Fan et al. [2011].

In Section 6.1, we consider (conditional) FDs, and we describe some results that have to do with the existence of good approximations, and obtaining approximations to minimal repairs. The "cleaning" process involved is based on changes of attribute values. In Section 6.2, we describe some approaches to database repairs, data cleaning, and consistent query answering for relational databases subject to uncertainty conditions.

6.1   DATA CLEANING AND QUERY ANSWERING FOR FD VIOLATIONS

Here, we describe some research on the problem of repairing an inconsistent database that violates a set of integrity constraints formed by conditional and classical functional dependencies. A repair is obtained by making the smallest possible *quantity of* modifications to the attribute values in the instance. At this point, the quantity can be just the number of changes or an aggregation of numerically weighted changes. This is a form of attribute-based repair as introduced in Section 5.8.

Since the repair process is based on making changes to attribute values in individual tuples, we need tuple identifiers, to refer to a tuple and its updated version in the repair. An instance D of relational schema is associated with a set of positions $Pos(D)$. Each position in $Pos(D)$ is of the form $p = (R, t, A)$, where R specifies relation name, t is a tuple identifier, and A is an attribute name. Then, $D(p)$ can be used to denote the value of $t[A]$ for the tuple identified by t in instance D.

For an inconsistent database instance D that violates a set of (conditional) FDs Σ, a repair is another instance D' with the same set of positions, but possibly different values stored in some

---

[1]Most frequently, the symbol $\rightleftharpoons$ is used instead of $\doteq$.

positions, that satisfies Σ.[2] The distance between instance D and a repair D', denoted by $d(D, D')$, is obtained by adding up the cost of updating the positions whose values have been changed in D'. That is,

$$d(D, D') = \sum_{p \in Pos(D), D(p) \neq D'(p)} w(p),$$

where $w(p)$ for position $p = (R, t, A)$ is the weight of making any update to tuple t. For example, it can represent the the level of confidence on the fact provided by t, or may be assigned to a default value, e.g., 1, if such information is not available. Then an *optimum repair* is a repair D^* that minimizes distance d.

The complexity of computing exact and approximate solutions to the optimum repair problem has been studied [Kolahi and Lakshmanan, 2009]. When approximating the optimum repair for an inconsistent instance D, we are typically looking for a (possibly non-optimum) repair D', such that $d(D, D') \leq \alpha \cdot d(D, D^*)$, for a small $\alpha > 1$. A related decision problem is about the existence of a consistent instance D' that approximates an optimum repair of D within a given factor. This is the *Approximating the Optimum Repair* decision problem. The results can be summarized as follows.

Theorem 6.2   [Kolahi and Lakshmanan, 2009] 1. There is a set of FDs Σ for which checking the existence of a repair D' with $d(D, D') \leq k$, for input instance D and $k > 0$, is *NP*-complete.
2. Let $\alpha > 1$ be any constant. The problem of approximating the optimum repair within a factor of α, with a set of FDs and an inconsistent instance as inputs, is *NP*-hard.
3. There is a set of FDs Σ and $\varepsilon > 0$, for which approximating the optimum repair within a factor of $(1 + \varepsilon)$ for an input instance D is *NP*-hard. That is, the optimum repair problem is *MAXSNP*-hard [Papadimitriou, 1994]. ∎

Despite the hardness results for approximations just presented, we briefly show here that, for a fixed set of FDs Σ, it is possible to generate a repair D' for an input instance D in polynomial time, such that $d(D, D') \leq \alpha_{\Sigma} \cdot d(D, D^*)$, for some $\alpha_{\Sigma} > 1$ that depends on the set of FDs.

For an instance D that violates a set of FDs Σ, a *basic conflict* is a subset-minimal set of positions $T \subseteq Pos(D)$, such that there is no repair D' of D, with $D(p) = D'(p)$ for every position $p \in T$. Intuitively, a basic conflicts shows a set of attribute values that cannot remain unchanged in any repair.

For instance, for $\Sigma = \{A \to C, B \to C\}$, the positions corresponding to the underlined values in the following instance form a basic conflict (assuming $c_2 \neq c_3$).

A	B	C
a_1	b_1	c_1
a_1	b_2	c_2
a_3	b_1	c_3

It is observed that, in general, the cardinality of a basic conflict can grow arbitrarily large [Kolahi and Lakshmanan, 2010]. However, under certain syntactic conditions on the set of

---

[2]Notice that in this section, a repair is just a consistent instance with the same positions as D. Minimality is explicitly stated when needed.

FDs, the cardinality of each basic conflict in any input instance is bounded by a constant α_Σ that depends on the set of FDs. As a consequence, the collection of basic conflicts can be computed in polynomial time in the size of the input instance.

It is also shown that, given a hitting set H for the collection of basic conflicts of an instance D (i.e., H is a subset-minimal set of positions that intersects with every basic conflict), it is possible to compute a repair D' that differs from D only in the values stored in positions in H.

These observations give us an approximation algorithm [Kolahi and Lakshmanan, 2010] for the optimum repair problem that works as follows:

1. Find the collection of basic conflicts in D.

2. Find an approximate solution H for the minimum hitting set of the collection of basic conflicts.

3. Find a repair D' by changing the values in H.

Notice that the minimum hitting set problem can be approximated within a constant factor α_Σ when the cardinality of each set in the collection is bounded by α_Σ.

Another approximation algorithm [Kolahi and Lakshmanan, 2009] starts by finding a subset of the basic conflicts in the inconsistent instance. After making changes to the positions in the (approximate) minimum hitting set, an extra step is required to take care of the remaining FD violations in such a way that the repair does not get far away from an optimum repair.

The notion of basic conflict has also been used for CQA, more specifically, for query answering over inconsistent databases that violate a set of (conditional) functional dependencies [Kolahi and Lakshmanan, 2010]. The conflict-aware query answering approach uses annotated databases and simple provenance management rules to *propagate* the basic conflicts in an inconsistent instance to the answer of a query.

After this propagation process, one checks whether a set of tuples in the query answer is created by a conflicting set of values, by looking at the provenance of the tuples. If the tuples do not contain traces of the basic conflicts, then they form a *possible answer*, meaning that they can be obtained from a minimal repair. For restricted classes of positive relational algebra queries, this approach can be used to precisely decide whether or not a given set of tuples in the answer can be obtained from running the query against one of the possibly many minimal repairs.

6.2   REPAIRS AND DATA CLEANING UNDER UNCERTAINTY

The quality of real world data is impaired by several errors and anomalies, such as duplicate records, violation of integrity constraints, and missing values. Most data cleaning approaches concentrate on producing a single clean database instance, i.e., a repair. However, the data cleaning process involves several uncertain aspects, e.g., uncertainty in determining whether two records are duplicates. Beskales et al. [2010] and Beskales et al. [2009] leverage the awareness of such uncertainty by adopting a probabilistic approach to data cleaning. Specifically, data cleaning is viewed as a probabilistic process whose possible outcomes are multiple possible repairs.

The concept of *uncertain data cleaning* has been applied in the context of two data quality problems: duplicate records elimination [Beskales et al., 2009], and violations of functional dependencies [Beskales et al., 2010].

6.2.1   UNCERTAIN DUPLICATE ELIMINATION

The goal of the duplicate elimination process is removing duplicate tuples from a given relation. More specifically, the duplicate elimination process is divided into two tasks: (1) identifying sets of tuples that refer to the same real-world entity; and (2) merging each set of such tuples into a single tuple. The outcome of the first stage is a clustering (i.e., partitioning) of tuples such that each cluster contains a set of tuples that are believed to be duplicates. In the second stage, members of each cluster are coalesced into a single representative tuple that replaces the member tuples in the relation. The result is a relation instance that is believed to be duplicate-free.

Due to the noise in real-world data, it is unlikely to find a perfect classifier that determines whether two tuples are duplicates, with no false positives or false negatives. To avoid information loss and degradation in data quality due to classification errors, Beskales et al. [2009] propose a framework that generates and stores a number of possible duplicate-free instances. That is, a set of possible clusterings are generated by the system, and their corresponding relation instances are compactly stored.

Considering all possible clusterings of tuples is both intractable (there may be exponentially many clusters in the relation size), and undesirable as many clusterings are very unlikely to be correct. Therefore, Beskales et al. [2009] propose an approach to constrain the space of possible clusterings: Given a parameterized clustering algorithm $\mathcal{A}$, they only consider clusterings that are valid outcomes of $\mathcal{A}$ using a set of possible parameter values. In other words, uncertainty in duplicate elimination process boils down to uncertainty in determining the most suitable value of the clustering algorithm parameter.

A family of clustering algorithms, namely hierarchical clustering algorithms [Jain and Dubes, 1988], exhibits some interesting properties that allow efficient generation of all possible instances for a range of possible parameter values. Hierarchical clustering algorithms cluster input tuples in a hierarchy, which represents a series of possible clusterings starting from a clustering containing each tuple in a separate cluster (the leafs level), to a clustering containing all tuples in one cluster (the root level). The algorithms use specific criteria, usually depending on a parameter, to determine which clustering to return. Given a range of possible parameter values, it is possible to generate all possible outcomes by invoking the clustering algorithm only once. The key idea is to use the maximum parameter value while constructing the clustering hierarchy, and capturing all clusterings that are encountered between the minimum and the maximum parameter values.

The instances corresponding to the generated clusterings are stored compactly by observing that each tuple in a duplicate-free instance also appears in a large number of instances. Therefore, each distinct tuple is stored only once, and annotated with metadata that captures the clustering algorithm parameter range in which such tuple is valid.

Given a set of possible instances, Beskales et al. [2009] define relational query answering, e.g., selection, projection, join and aggregation, according to the *possible worlds semantics* [Dalvi and Suciu, 2007]. Query processing is implemented using a query rewriting mechanism. That is, each relational query is modified to correctly handle the special metadata associated with tuples. An efficient algorithm is proposed to further reduce the complexity of answering aggregate queries. Moreover, new query types that directly reason about uncertainty in the duplicate elimination process are proposed, e.g., obtaining the most probable instance, obtaining the tuples that are almost certain to appear in a duplicate-free instance, and obtaining the probability that a pair of input tuples are duplicates.

6.2.2   UNCERTAIN REPAIRING OF FD VIOLATIONS

Assume that a set, Σ, of FDs is defined over a relational database schema. Repairing a database instance that violates Σ can be achieved by performing a number of modifications to tuple attribute values such that the resulting instance, called a repair, satisfies the FDs.

Repairing a given data instance with respect to Σ can be done in several ways. For example, assume that tuples t_i and t_j violate $A \rightarrow B$. It is possible to fix such violation by changing the value of attribute B in t_i, i.e., $t_i[B]$, to be equal to $t_j[B]$, or vice versa. Alternatively, it is possible to change the value of attribute A of t_i to be different from $t_j[A]$, or vice versa. Several approaches aim at generating a repair that involves the smallest number of changes [Bohannon et al., 2005, Kolahi and Lakshmanan, 2009] (cf. Section 6.1). The main hypothesis behind such minimality constraint is that the largest part of the data is clean, and thus we only need to perform a number of data changes that is relatively small compared to the data size. The related and sometimes alternative approach of Consistent Query Answering can be applied: it defines a set of possible repairs, and focus on obtaining query answers that are correct in every possible repair in an efficient way (cf. Chapter 3).

A third approach, proposed by Beskales et al. [2010], is to obtain a random sample of repairs and use such sample to answer user queries. That is, an algorithm is provided to efficiently generate a repair that is selected at random from the sampling population. The minimality of the number of changes in sampled repairs is abandoned to avoid reducing the scope of the possible repairs. However, each generated repair is guaranteed to consists of necessary changes only. That is, if a generated repair consists of a set of assignments $\{t_i[A_j] := v_{ij}\}$, any subset of the assignments does not represent a repair. Additionally, the sampling population is proved to contain all *cardinality-set-minimal* repairs (as they are called by Beskales et al. [2010]). These are attribute-based repairs (cf. Section 5.8) that minimize wrt set inclusion the set of changed tuple attribute values (also called, *cells*). That is, a repair that changes a set of cells S is cardinality-set-minimal if there does not exist another repair that changes a subset of S.

The sampling algorithm is based on maintaining a set of cells that are consistent with Σ, in the sense that it is possible to find an instance that satisfies Σ without changing such cells. Initially, the set of consistent cells, denoted CL, is equal to the empty set, $\emptyset$. The algorithm iteratively selects a random cell c and checks whether $CL \cup \{c\}$ is consistent with Σ. If that is not the case, the value of

c is changed to c' in such a way that $CL \cup \{c'\}$ is consistent. The cell c' is inserted into CL, and the algorithm proceeds by selecting another cell. The algorithm terminates when all cells are inserted in CL and return the constructed instance.

Beskales et al. [2010] describe a method to improve the efficiency of the sampling algorithm by initially partitioning the input database instance into blocks that can be repaired independently. Blocks consisting of single cells, which are frequently found in practice, are consistent with Σ, and thus are not considered by the repairing algorithm.

A modified version of the sampling algorithm has been proposed to allow specifying additional user constraints that prevent changing parts of the database. Those constraints become *hard constraints* and are useful in various scenarios. For example, if data in an input relation is collected from two different sources, one of which is completely trusted, then it is possible to specify such knowledge using the provided functionality. The algorithm is modified to respect such constraints by initially setting CL to the set of cells that should not be altered, and proceeding as before. Another use of hard constraints was described in Section 5.8.

Bibliography

S. Abiteboul, R. Hull, and V. Vianu. *Foundations of Databases*. Addison-Wesley, 1995. Cited on page(s) 2, 6, 11, 20, 35, 53, 58, 59, 60

F. Afrati and Ph. Kolaities. Answering Aggregate Queries in Data Exchange. In *Proc. ACM SIGACT-SIGMOD Symp. on Principles of Database Systems*, pages 129–138, 2008. DOI: 10.1080/19463138.2011.583530 Cited on page(s) 65

F. Afrati and Ph. Kolaitis. Repair Checking in Inconsistent Databases: Algorithms and Complexity. In *Proc. 12th Int. Conf. on Database Theory*, pages 31–41, 2009. DOI: 10.1177/0956247806069608 Cited on page(s) 18, 21, 56, 71, 85

P. Andritsos, A. Fuxman, and R. Miller. Clean Answers over Dirty Databases: A Probabilistic Approach. In *Proc. 22nd Int. Conf. on Data Engineering*, 2006. DOI: 10.1109/ICDE.2006.35 Cited on page(s) xiv

M. Arenas and L. Bertossi. On the Decidability of Consistent Query Answering. In *Proc. Alberto Mendelzon Int. Workshop on Foundations of Data Management*. CEUR Proceedings, Vol. 619, 2010. DOI: 10.1080/00049180500511962 Cited on page(s) 61, 62, 64

M. Arenas, L. Bertossi, and J. Chomicki. Consistent Query Answers in Inconsistent Databases. In *Proc. 18th ACM SIGACT-SIGMOD-SIGART Symp. on Principles of Database Systems*, pages 53–62, 1999. DOI: 10.1145/303976.303983 Cited on page(s) xiii, 4, 5, 13, 14, 16, 23, 24, 25, 26, 27, 58, 81, 85

M. Arenas, L. Bertossi, and M. Kifer. Applications of Annotated Predicate Calculus to Querying Inconsistent Databases. In *Proc. 6th Int. Conf. on Deductive and Object-Oriented Databases*, pages 926–941. Springer LNCS 1861, 2000. DOI: 10.1007/s002679900032 Cited on page(s) 35, 45, 47

M. Arenas, L. Bertossi, and J. Chomicki. Scalar Aggregation in FD-Inconsistent Databases. In *Proc. 8th Int. Conf. on Database Theory*, pages 39–53, 2001. Cited on page(s) 29

M. Arenas, L. Bertossi, and J. Chomicki. Answer Sets for Consistent Query Answering in Inconsistent Databases. *Theory and Practice of Logic Programming*, 3(4-5):393–424, 2003a. DOI: 10.1017/S1471068403001832 Cited on page(s) 18, 35, 37, 67, 71, 81

M. Arenas, L. Bertossi, J. Chomicki, X. He, V. Raghavan, and J. Spinrad. Scalar Aggregation in Inconsistent Databases. *Theor. Comput. Sci.*, 296(3):405–434, 2003b. DOI: 10.1016/S0304-3975(02)00737-5 Cited on page(s) 15, 29, 56, 64, 65, 66, 81

O. Arieli, M. Denecker, B. Van Nuffelen, and M. Bruynooghe. Computational Methods for Database Repair by Signed Formulae. *Ann. Math. Artif. Intell.*, 46(1-2):4–37, 2006. DOI: 10.1007/s10472-005-9012-z Cited on page(s) 18, 34

S. Ariyan and L. Bertossi. Structural Repairs of Multidimensional Databases. In *Proc. Alberto Mendelzon Int. Workshop of Foundations of Data Management*. CEUR Proceedings, Vol. 619, 2011. DOI: 10.2166/ws.2008.104 Cited on page(s) xiv

Ch. Baral. *Knowledge Representation, Reasoning and Declarative Problem Solving*. Cambridge University Press, 2003. Cited on page(s) 34, 85

P. Barceló and L. Bertossi. Repairing Databases with Annotated Predicate Logic. In *Proc. Int. Workshop on Non-Monotonic Reasoning*, 2002. Cited on page(s) 47, 48

P. Barceló and L. Bertossi. Logic Programs for Querying Inconsistent Databases. In *Proc. Practical Aspects of Declarative Languages*, pages 208–222. Springer LNCS 2562, 2003. Cited on page(s) 35

P. Barceló, L. Bertossi, and L. Bravo. Characterizing and Computing Semantically Correct Answers from Databases with Annotated Logic and Answer Sets. In L. Bertossi, G.O.H. Katona, K.-D. Schewe, and B. Thalheim, editors, *Semantics in Databases*, pages 7–33. Springer LNCS 2582, 2003. Cited on page(s) 35, 47, 48, 56

C. Beeri, R. Fagin, D. Maier, and M. Yannakakis. On the Desirability of Acyclic Database Schemes. *J. ACM*, 30:479–513, 1983. DOI: 10.1145/2402.322389 Cited on page(s) 32, 59

O. Benjelloun, H. Garcia-Molina, D. Menestrina, Q. Su, S. Euijong Whang, and J. Widom. Swoosh: A Generic Approach to Entity Resolution. *VLDB J.*, 18(1):255–276, 2009. DOI: 10.1007/s00778-008-0098-x Cited on page(s) 86

L. Bertossi. Consistent Query Answering in Databases. *ACM SIGMOD Rec.*, 35(2):68–76, 2006. DOI: 10.1145/1147376.1147391 Cited on page(s) xiv

L. Bertossi. From Database Repair Programs to Consistent Query Answering in Classical Logic. In *Proc. Alberto Mendelzon Int. Workshop on Foundations of Data Management*. CEUR Proceedings, Vol. 450, 2009. Cited on page(s) 48, 49

L. Bertossi and L. Bravo. Query Answering in Peer-to-Peer Data Exchange Systems. In *Proc. Int. Workshop on Peer-to-Peer Computing & DataBases*, pages 478–485. Springer LNCS 3268, 2004a. DOI: 10.1007/978-3-540-30192-9_47 Cited on page(s) xiv

L. Bertossi and L. Bravo. Consistent Query Answers in Virtual Data Integration Systems. In L. Bertossi, A. Hunter, and T. Schaub, editors, *Inconsistency Tolerance*, pages 42–83. Springer LNCS 3300, 2004b. Cited on page(s) xiv

L. Bertossi and L. Bravo. The Semantics of Consistency and Trust in Peer Data Exchange Systems. In *Proc. Int. Conf. on Logic for Programming, Artificial Intelligence, and Reasoning*, pages 107–122. Springer LNCS 4790, 2007. DOI: 10.1007/978-3-540-75560-9_10 Cited on page(s) xiv, 18, 42, 44

L. Bertossi and L. Bravo. Information Sharing Agents in a Peer Data Exchange System. In *Proc. Int. Conf. on Data Management in Grid and P2P Systems*, pages 70–81. Springer LNCS 5187, 2008. DOI: 10.1007/978-3-540-85176-9_7 Cited on page(s) xiv

L. Bertossi and J. Chomicki. Query Answering in Inconsistent Databases. In J. Chomicki, G. Saake, and R. Van der Meyden, editors, *Logics for Emerging Applications of Databases*, pages 43–83. Springer, 2003. Cited on page(s) xiv

L. Bertossi and L. Li. Achieving Data Privacy through Secrecy Views and Null-Based Virtual Updates. 2011. Corr ArXiv paper cs.DB/1105.1364. DOI: 10.1038/387253a0 Cited on page(s) 19, 44

L. Bertossi and C. Schwind. Database Repairs and Analytic Tableaux. *Ann. Math. Artif. Intell.*, 40 (1-2):5–35, 2004. DOI: 10.1016/S0140-6736(09)60935-1 Cited on page(s) 34

L. Bertossi, L. Bravo, E. Franconi, and A. Lopatenko. The Complexity and Approximation of Fixing Numerical Attributes in Databases under Integrity Constraints. *Inf. Syst.*, 33(4-5):407–434, 2008. DOI: 10.1016/j.is.2008.01.005 Cited on page(s) 19, 29, 67, 73, 74, 75, 76, 78, 84

L. Bertossi, L. Bravo, and M. Caniupan. Consistent Query Answering in Data Warehouses. In *Proc. The Alberto Mendelzon Int. Workshop on Foundations of Data Management*. CEUR Proceedings, Vol-450, 2009. Cited on page(s) xiv

L. Bertossi, S. Kolahi, and L. Lakshmanan. Data Cleaning and Query Answering with Matching Dependencies and Matching Functions. In *Proc. 14th Int. Conf. on Database Theory*, 2011. DOI: 10.1145/1938551.1938585 Cited on page(s) 87

G. Beskales, M. Soliman, I. Ilyas, and S. Ben-David. Modeling and Querying Possible Repairs in Duplicate Detection. *Proc. 35th Int. Conf. on Very Large Data Bases*, 2(1):598–609, 2009. Cited on page(s) 89, 90, 91

G. Beskales, I. Ilyas, and L. Golab. Sampling the Repairs of Functional Dependency Violations under Hard Constraints. *Proc. 36th Int. Conf. on Very Large Data Bases*, 3(1):197–207, 2010. DOI: 10.1006/jema.1993.1044 Cited on page(s) 89, 90, 91, 92

J. Bleiholder and F. Naumann. Data Fusion. *ACM Comput. Surv.*, 41(1), 2008. Cited on page(s) 86

Ph. Bohannon, M. Flaster, W. Fan, and R. Rastogi. A Cost-Based Model and Effective Heuristic for Repairing Constraints by Value Modification. In *Proc. ACM SIGMOD Int. Conf. on Management of Data*, pages 143–154, 2005. DOI: 10.1145/1066157.1066175 Cited on page(s) 19, 72, 73, 85, 91

E. Börger, E. Grädel, and Y. Gurevich. *The Classical Decision Problem*. Springer, 2001. Cited on page(s) 62, 64

L. Bravo and L. Bertossi. Logic Programs for Consistently Querying Data Integration Systems. In *Proc. 18th Int. Joint Conf. on AI*, pages 10–15. Morgan Kaufmann, 2003. Cited on page(s) xiv

L. Bravo and L. Bertossi. Disjunctive Deductive Databases for Computing Certain and Consistent Answers to Queries from Mediated Data Integration Systems. *J. Applied Logic*, 3(2):329–367, 2005. DOI: 10.1016/j.jal.2004.07.023 Cited on page(s) xiv

L. Bravo and L. Bertossi. Semantically Correct Query Answers in the Presence of Null Values. In *EDBT Workshops*, pages 336–357. Springer LNCS 4254, 2006. DOI: 10.1007/11896548_27 Cited on page(s) 18, 35, 42, 43, 44, 59

L. Bravo, W. Fan, and S. Ma. Extending Dependencies with Conditions. In *Proc. 33rd Int. Conf. on Very Large Data Bases*, pages 243–254, 2007. Cited on page(s) 85

L. Bravo, M. Caniupan, and Hurtado C. Logic Programs for Repairing Inconsistent Dimensions in Data Warehouses. In *Proc. The Alberto Mendelzon Int. Workshop on Foundations of Data Management*. CEUR Proceedings, Vol-619, 2010. DOI: 10.1016/j.respol.2006.06.001 Cited on page(s) xiv

F. Buccafurri, N. Leone, and P. Rullo. Enhancing Disjunctive Datalog by Constraints. *IEEE Trans. Knowl. and Data Eng.*, 12(5):845–860, 2000. DOI: 10.1109/69.877512 Cited on page(s) 71, 72

A. Calì, D. Lembo, and R. Rosati. On the Decidability and Complexity of Query Answering over Inconsistent and Incomplete Databases. In *Proc. 22nd ACM SIGACT-SIGMOD-SIGART Symp. on Principles of Database Systems*, pages 260–271, 2003. DOI: 10.1145/773153.773179 Cited on page(s) 17, 18, 44, 58, 60

F. Calimeri, W. Faber, G. Pfeifer, and N. Leone. Pruning Operators for Disjunctive Logic Programming Systems. *Fundamenta Informaticae*, 71(2-3):183–214, 2006. Cited on page(s) 39

M. Caniupan and L. Bertossi. The Consistency Extractor System: Answer Set Programs for Consistent Query Answering in Databases. *Data & Knowl. Eng.*, 69(6):545–572, 2010. DOI: 10.1016/j.datak.2010.01.005 Cited on page(s) 35, 37, 38, 39, 40, 44

A. Celle and L. Bertossi. Querying Inconsistent Databases: Algorithms and Implementation. In *Proc. 6th Int. Conf. on Deductive and Object-Oriented Databases*, pages 942–956. Springer LNCS 1861, 2000. Cited on page(s) 28, 32

S. Ceri, G. Gottlob, and L. Tanca. *Logic Programming and Databases*. Springer, 1989. Cited on page(s) 6, 35, 38

S. Chakravarthy, John Grant, and Jack Minker. Logic-Based Approach to Semantic Query Optimization. *ACM Trans. Database Syst.*, 15(2):162, 1990. DOI: 10.1145/78922.78924 Cited on page(s) 24

J. Chomicki. Consistent Query Answering: Five Easy Pieces. In *Proc. 11th Int. Conf. on Database Theory*, pages 1–17. Springer LNCS 4353, 2007. DOI: 10.1007/11965893_1 Cited on page(s) xiv

J. Chomicki and J. Marcinkowski. Minimal-Change Integrity Maintenance Using Tuple Deletions. *Information and Comput.*, 197(1-2):90–121, 2005. DOI: 10.1080/714038561 Cited on page(s) 17, 28, 29, 30, 31, 56, 57, 58, 71

J. Chomicki, J. Marcinkowski, and S. Staworko. Computing Consistent Query Answers using Conflict Hypergraphs. In *Proc. Int. Conf. on Information and Knowledge Management*, pages 417–426, 2004. DOI: 10.1145/1031171.1031254 Cited on page(s) 30, 32

V. Chvatal. A Greedy Heuristic for the Set Covering Problem. *Math. Oper. Res.*, 4:233–235, 1979. DOI: 10.1287/moor.4.3.233 Cited on page(s) 78

E.F. Codd. A Relational Model of Data for Large Shared Data Banks. *Commun. ACM*, 13(6): 377–387, 1970. DOI: 10.1145/357980.358007 Cited on page(s) 1

C. Cumbo, W. Faber, G. Greco, and N. Leone. Enhancing the Magic-Set Method for Disjunctive Datalog Programs. In *Proc. 20th Int. Conf. Logic Programming*, pages 371–385, 2004. DOI: 10.1007/978-3-540-27775-0_26 Cited on page(s) 39

N. Dalvi and D. Suciu. Efficient Query Evaluation on Probabilistic Databases. *VLDB J.*, 16(4): 523–544, 2007. DOI: 10.1007/s00778-006-0004-3 Cited on page(s) 91

E. Dantsin, T. Eiter, G. Gottlob, and A. Voronkov. Complexity and Expressive Power of Logic Programming. *ACM Comput. Surv.*, 33(3):374–425, 2001. DOI: 10.1145/502807.502810 Cited on page(s) 35, 54, 56

P. Doherty, W. Lukaszewicz, and A. Szalas. Computing Circumscription Revisited: A Reduction Algorithm. *J. Autom. Reasoning*, 18(3):297–336, 1997. DOI: 10.1023/A:1005722130532 Cited on page(s) 49, 50

H.-D. Ebbinghaus and J. Flum. *Finite Model Theory*. Springer, 2 edition, 2005. Cited on page(s) 59

98 BIBLIOGRAPHY

H.-D. Ebbinghaus, J. Flum, and W. Thomas. *Mathematical Logic*. Springer, 2 edition, 1994. Cited on page(s) 59

T. Eiter and G. Gottlob. On the Complexity of Propositional Knowledge Base Revision, Updates, and Counterfactuals. *Artif. Intell.*, 57(2-3):227–270, 1992. DOI: 10.1145/137097.137886 Cited on page(s) 56, 81

T. Eiter, G. Gottlob, and H. Mannila. Disjunctive Datalog. *ACM Trans. Database Syst.*, 22(3): 364–418, 1997. DOI: 10.1145/261124.261126 Cited on page(s) 34

T. Eiter, M. Fink, G. Greco, and D. Lembo. Repair Localization for Query Answering from Inconsistent Databases. *ACM Trans. Database Syst.*, 33(2), 2008. DOI: 10.1145/1366102.1366107 Cited on page(s) 37, 38

A. Elmagarmid, P. Ipeirotis, and V. Verykios. Duplicate Record Detection: A Survey. *IEEE Trans. Knowl. and Data Eng.*, 19(1):1–16, 2007. DOI: 10.1109/TKDE.2007.250581 Cited on page(s) 86

H. Enderton. *A Mathematical Introduction to Logic*. Academic Press, 2 edition, 2001. Cited on page(s) 2, 3

W. Faber, G. Greco, and N. Leone. Magic Sets and Their Application to Data Integration. *J. Comp. and System Sci.*, 73(4):584–609, 2007. DOI: 10.1007/978-3-540-30570-5_21 Cited on page(s) 39

W. Fan. Dependencies Revisited for Improving Data Quality. In *Proc. ACM SIGACT-SIGMOD Symp. on Principles of Database Systems*, pages 159–170, 2008. DOI: 10.1145/1376916.1376940 Cited on page(s) 85, 86

W. Fan, F. Geerts, X. Jia, and A. Kementsietsidis. Conditional Functional Dependencies for Capturing Data Inconsistencies. *ACM Trans. Database Syst.*, 33(2), 2008. DOI: 10.1145/1366102.1366103 Cited on page(s) 85

W. Fan, X. Jia, J. Li, and S. Ma. Reasoning about Record Matching Rules. *Proc. 35th Int. Conf. on Very Large Data Bases*, 2(1):407–418, 2009. Cited on page(s) 86, 87

W. Fan, J. Li, S. Ma, N. Tang, and W. Yu. Towards Certain Fixes with Editing Rules and Master Data. *Proc. 36th Int. Conf. on Very Large Data Bases*, 3(1):173–184, 2010. Cited on page(s) 85

W. Fan, J. Li, S. Ma, N. Tang, and W. Yu. Interaction between Record Matching and Data Repairing. In *Proc. ACM SIGMOD Int. Conf. on Management of Data*, 2011. DOI: 10.1145/1989323.1989373 Cited on page(s) 87

P. Ferraris, J. Lee, and V. Lifschitz. Stable Models and Circumscription. *Artif. Intell.*, 175(1): 236–263, 2011. DOI: 10.1016/j.artint.2010.04.011 Cited on page(s) 48, 49

S. Flesca, F. Furfaro, S. Greco, and E. Zumpano. Querying and Repairing Inconsistent XML Data. In *Proc. Web Information Systems Engineering*, pages 175–188. Springer LNCS 3806, 2005a. DOI: 10.1007/11581062_14 Cited on page(s) xiv

S. Flesca, F. Furfaro, S. Greco, and E. Zumpano. Repairing Inconsistent XML Data with Functional Dependencies. In L. Rivero, J. Doorn, and V. Ferraggine, editors, *Encyclopedia of Database Technologies and Applications*, pages 542–547. Idea Group, 2005b. DOI: 10.4018/978-1-59140-560-3.ch090 Cited on page(s) xiv

S. Flesca, F. Furfaro, and F. Parisi. Querying and Repairing Inconsistent Numerical Databases. *ACM Trans. Database Syst.*, 35(2), 2010a. DOI: 10.1145/1735886.1735893 Cited on page(s) 19, 67, 80, 81

S. Flesca, F. Furfaro, and F. Parisi. Range-Consistent Answers of Aggregate Queries under Aggregate Constraints. In *Proc. Int. Conf. on Scalable Uncertainty Management*, pages 163–176. Springer LNCS 6379, 2010b. DOI: 10.1007/978-3-642-15951-0_19 Cited on page(s) 80, 81

J. Flum and M. Grohe. *Parameterized Complexity Theory*. Texts in Theoretical Computer Science. Springer, 2006. Cited on page(s) 82

E. Franconi, A. Laureti-Palma, N. Leone, S. Perri, and F. Scarcello. Census Data Repair: A Challenging Application of Disjunctive Logic Programming. In *Proc. Int. Conf. on Logic for Programming, Artificial Intelligence, and Reasoning*, pages 561–578. Springer LNCS 2250, 2001. DOI: 10.1177/0956247808089149 Cited on page(s) 19, 72, 76

A. Fuxman and R. Miller. Towards Inconsistency Management in Data Integration Systems. In *Proc. Workshop on Information Integration on the Web*, pages 143–148, 2003. Cited on page(s) 59

A. Fuxman and R. Miller. First-Order Query Rewriting for Inconsistent Databases. In *Proc. 10th Int. Conf. on Database Theory*, pages 337–351, 2005. Cited on page(s) 31, 60

A. Fuxman and R. Miller. First-Order Query Rewriting for Inconsistent Databases. *J. Comp. and System Sci.*, 73(4):610–635, 2007. DOI: 10.1016/j.jcss.2006.10.013 Cited on page(s) 28, 31, 32, 60

A. Fuxman, E. Fazli, and R. Miller. ConQuer: Efficient Management of Inconsistent Databases. In *Proc. ACM SIGMOD Int. Conf. on Management of Data*, pages 155–166, 2005. DOI: 10.1145/1066157.1066176 Cited on page(s) 32, 67

J. Gardezi, L. Bertossi, and I. Kiringa. Matching Dependencies with Arbitrary Attribute Values: Semantics, Query Answering and Integrity Constraints. In *Proc. Int. Workshop on Logic in Databases*. ACM Press, 2011. DOI: 10.1145/1966357.1966362 Cited on page(s) 87

M. Gelfond and N. Leone. Logic Programming and Knowledge Representation - The A-Prolog Perspective. *Artif. Intell.*, 138(1-2):3–38, 2002. DOI: 10.1016/S0004-3702(02)00207-2 Cited on page(s) 34, 85

M. Gelfond and V. Lifschitz. Logic Programs with Classical Negation. In *Proc. 7th Int. Conf. Logic Programming*, pages 579–597, 1990. Cited on page(s) 34

M. Gelfond and V. Lifschitz. Classical Negation in Logic Programs and Disjunctive Databases. *New Generation Comput.*, 9(3/4):365–386, 1991. DOI: 10.1007/BF03037169 Cited on page(s) 34

F. Giannotti, S. Greco, D. Saccà, and C. Zaniolo. Programming with Non-Determinism in Deductive Databases. *Ann. Math. Artif. Intell.*, 19(1-2), 1997. DOI: 10.1023/A:1018899404360 Cited on page(s) 42

G. Greco, S. Greco, and E. Zumpano. A Logical Framework for Querying and Repairing Inconsistent Databases. *IEEE Trans. Knowl. and Data Eng.*, 15(6):1389–1408, 2003. DOI: 10.1006/jema.1996.0044 Cited on page(s) 35

L. Grieco, D. Lembo, R. Rosati, and M. Ruzzi. Consistent Query Answering under Key and Exclusion Dependencies: Algorithms and Experiments. In *Proc. Int. Conf. on Information and Knowledge Management*, pages 792–799, 2005. DOI: 10.1145/1099554.1099742 Cited on page(s) 29, 32

D. Hochbaum, editor. *Approximation Algorithms for NP-Hard Problems*. PWS, 1997. Cited on page(s) 78

C. Hurtado and A. Mendelzon. OLAP Dimension Constraints. In *Proc. 21st ACM SIGACT-SIGMOD-SIGART Symp. on Principles of Database Systems*, pages 169–179, 2002. DOI: 10.1080/10304310500322685 Cited on page(s) xiv

T. Imielinski and W. Lipski. Incomplete Information in Relational Databases. *J. ACM*, 31(4): 761–791, 1984. DOI: 10.1145/1634.1886 Cited on page(s) 14

A. Jain and R. Dubes. *Algorithms for Clustering Data*. Prentice-Hall, 1988. Cited on page(s) 90

D.S. Johnson. A Catalog of Complexity Classes. In *Handbook of Theoretical Computer Science, Vol. A*, pages 67–161. Elsevier, 1990. Cited on page(s) 54, 55

M. Kifer and E. Lozinskii. A Logic for Reasoning with Inconsistency. *J. Autom. Reasoning*, 9(2): 179–215, 1992. DOI: 10.1007/BF00245460 Cited on page(s) 45, 47

S. Kolahi and L. Lakshmanan. On Approximating Optimum Repairs for Functional Dependency Violations. In *Proc. 12th Int. Conf. on Database Theory*, pages 53–62, 2009. DOI: 10.1145/1514894.1514901 Cited on page(s) 86, 88, 89, 91

S. Kolahi and L. Lakshmanan. Exploiting Conflict Structures in Inconsistent Databases. In *Proc. Advances in Databases and Information Systems*, pages 320–335. Springer LNCS 6295, 2010. DOI: 10.1007/978-3-642-15576-5_25 Cited on page(s) 86, 88, 89

M. Krentel. The Complexity of Optimization Problems. *J. Comp. and System Sci.*, 36:490–509, 1988. DOI: 10.1145/12130.12138 Cited on page(s) 70, 71, 83

N. Leone, G. Pfeifer, W. Faber, T. Eiter, G. Gottlob, S. Perri, and F. Scarcello. The DLV System for Knowledge Representation and Reasoning. *ACM Trans. Comput. Log.*, 7 (3):499–562, 2006. DOI: 10.1145/1149114.1149117 Cited on page(s) 37

X. Lian, L. Chen, and S. Song. Consistent Query Answers in Inconsistent Probabilistic Databases. In *Proc. ACM SIGMOD Int. Conf. on Management of Data*, pages 303–314, 2010. DOI: 10.1145/1807167.1807202 Cited on page(s) xiv

L. Libkin. *Elements of Finite Model Theory*. Springer, 2004. Cited on page(s) 59

L. Libkin. The Finite Model Theory Toolbox of a Database Theoretician. In *Proc. ACM SIGACT-SIGMOD Symp. on Principles of Database Systems*, pages 65–76, 2009. DOI: 10.1145/1559795.1559807 Cited on page(s) 59

V. Lifschitz. Circumscription. In *Handbook of Logic in Artificial Intelligence and Logic Programming, Vol. 3*, pages 297–352. Oxford University Press, 1994. Cited on page(s) 48, 49

J. Lloyd. *Foundations of Logic Programming*. Springer, 2 edition, 1987. Cited on page(s) 23, 38, 46, 49, 54

A. Lopatenko and L. Bertossi. Complexity of Consistent Query Answering in Databases Under Cardinality-Based and Incremental Repair Semantics. In *Proc. 11th Int. Conf. on Database Theory*, pages 179–193, 2007. DOI: 10.1126/science.155.3767.1203 Cited on page(s) 18, 19, 21, 29, 68, 70, 71, 81, 82, 83

A. Lopatenko and L. Bravo. Efficient Approximation Algorithms for Repairing Inconsistent Databases. In *Proc. 19th Int. Conf. on Data Engineering*, pages 216–225, 2003. DOI: 10.1109/ICDE.2007.367867 Cited on page(s) 78

J.A. Makowsky. From Hilbert's Program to a Logic Tool Box. *Ann. Math. Artif. Intell.*, 53(1-4): 225–250, 2008. DOI: 10.1007/s10472-009-9115-z Cited on page(s) 59

J. McCarthy. Circumscription - A Form of Non-Monotonic Reasoning. *Artif. Intell.*, 13(1-2):27–39, 1980. DOI: 10.1016/0004-3702(80)90011-9 Cited on page(s) 48

C. Molinaro and S. Greco. Polynomial Time Queries over Inconsistent Databases with Functional Dependencies and Foreign Keys. *Data & Knowl. Eng.*, 69:709–722, 2010. DOI: 10.1016/j.datak.2010.02.007 Cited on page(s) 18

C. Molinaro, J. Chomicki, and J. Marcinkowski. Disjunctive Databases for Representing Repairs. *Ann. Math. Artif. Intell.*, 57(2):103–124, 2009. DOI: 10.1007/s10472-009-9159-0   Cited on page(s) 34

R. Niedermeier and P. Rossmanith. An Efficient Fixed-Parameter Algorithm for 3-Hitting Set. *J. Discrete Algorithms*, 1(1):89–102, 2003. DOI: 10.1016/S1570-8667(03)00009-1 Cited on page(s) 82

Ch. Papadimitriou. *Computational Complexity*. Addison Wesley, 1994. Cited on page(s) 54, 76, 88

E. Pema, Ph. Kolaitis, and W.-Ch. Tan. On the Tractability and Intractability of Consistent Conjunctive Query Answering. In *Proc. 2011 Joint EDBT/ICDT Ph.D. Workshop*, pages 38–44. ACM Press, 2011. DOI: 10.1145/1966874.1966881 Cited on page(s) 59, 60

R. Reiter. Towards a Logical Reconstruction of Relational Database Theory. In M. Brodie, J. Mylopoulos, and J. Schmidt, editors, *On Conceptual Modelling*, pages 191—-233. Springer, 1984. Cited on page(s) 45, 49

A. Rodriguez, L. Bertossi, and M. Caniupan. An Inconsistency Tolerant Approach to Querying Spatial Databases. In *Proc. 16th ACM SIGSPATIAL Int. Symp. on Advances in Geographic Information Systems*, 2008. DOI: 10.1145/1463434.1463480 Cited on page(s) xiv

A. Rodriguez, L. Bertossi, and M. Caniupan. Consistent Query Answering under Spatial Semantic Constraints. 2011. Corr ArXiv paper cs.DB/1106.1478. Cited on page(s) xiv

K. Sagonas, T. Swift, and D.S. Warren. XSB as an Efficient Deductive Database Engine. In *Proc. ACM SIGMOD Int. Conf. on Management of Data*, pages 442–453, 1994. DOI: 10.1145/191839.191927 Cited on page(s) 28

S. Staworko and J. Chomicki. Validity-Sensitive Querying of XML Databases. In *EDBT Workshops*, pages 164–177. Springer LNCS 4254, 2006. DOI: 10.1007/11896548_16 Cited on page(s) xiv

S. Staworko and J. Chomicki. Consistent Query Answers in the Presence of Universal Constraints. *Inf. Syst.*, 35(1):1–22, 2010. DOI: 10.1016/j.is.2009.03.004 Cited on page(s) 30, 58

M. Vardi. The Complexity of Relaitonal Query Languages. In *Proc. 14th Annual ACM Symp. on Theory of Computing*, pages 137–146. ACM Press, 1982. DOI: 10.1145/800070.802186 Cited on page(s) 53

J. Wijsen. Database Repairing Using Updates. *ACM Trans. Database Syst.*, 30(3):722–768, 2005. DOI: 10.1145/1093382.1093385 Cited on page(s) 19, 72

J. Wijsen. Project-Join-Repair: An Approach to Consistent Query Processing under Funtional Dependencies. In *Proc. 7th Int. Conf. Flexible Query Answering Systems*, pages 1–12. Springer LNAI 4027, 2006. Cited on page(s) 19, 20, 21

J. Wijsen.   Consistent Query Answering under Primary Keys: A Characterization of Tractable Queries. In *Proc. 12th Int. Conf. on Database Theory*, pages 42–52, 2009a. DOI: 10.1145/1514894.1514900 Cited on page(s) 29

J. Wijsen. On the Consistent Rewriting of Conjunctive Queries under Primary Key Constraints. *Inf. Syst.*, 34(7):578–601, 2009b. DOI: 10.1016/j.is.2009.03.011 Cited on page(s) 29, 31, 32, 59

J. Wijsen. A Remark on the Complexity of Consistent Conjunctive Query Answering under Primary Key Violations. *Inf. Proc. Letters*, 110(21):950–955, 2010a. DOI: 10.1016/j.ipl.2010.07.021 Cited on page(s) 60

J. Wijsen. On the First-Order Expressibility of Computing Certain Answers to Conjunctive Queries over Uncertain Databases. In *Proc. ACM SIGACT-SIGMOD Symp. on Principles of Database Systems*, pages 179–190, 2010b. DOI: 10.1145/1807085.1807111 Cited on page(s) 59, 60

Author's Biography

LEOPOLDO BERTOSSI

Leopoldo Bertossi has been Full Professor at the School of Computer Science, Carleton University (Ottawa, Canada) since 2001. He is Faculty Fellow of the IBM Center for Advanced Studies. He obtained a Ph.D. in Mathematics from the Pontifical Catholic University of Chile (PUC) in 1988.

He has been the theme leader for "Adaptive Data Quality and Data Cleaning" of the "NSERC Strategic Network for Data Management for Business Intelligence" (BIN), an ongoing umbrella research project that involves more than 15 academic researchers across Canada plus several industrial partners.

Until 2001 he was professor and departmental chair (1993–1995) at the Department of Computer Science, PUC, and was also the President of the Chilean Computer Science Society (SCCC) in 1996 and 1999–2000.

He has been visiting professor at the computer science departments of the universities of Toronto (1989/90), Wisconsin-Milwaukee (1990/91), Marseille-Luminy (1997) and visiting researcher at the Technical University Berlin (1997/98), visiting researcher and professor at the Free University of Bolzano-Bozen (Italy). In 2006, he was a visiting researcher at the Technical University of Vienna as a Pauli Fellow of the "Wolfgang Pauli Institute (WPI) Vienna".

Prof. Bertossi's research interests include database theory, data integration, peer data management, semantic web, intelligent information systems, data quality for business intelligence, knowledge representation, logic programming, and computational logic.